THE
ART of
LISTENING

INTUITION & IMPROVISATION IN CHOREOGRAPHY

DARLA JOHNSON

Publishing

Copyright © 2012 Darla Johnson

ISBN 978-1-934302-93-4 (softback)

TSTC Publishing
Texas State Technical College Waco
3801 Campus Drive
Waco, Texas 76705

publishing.tstc.edu

Publisher: Mark Long
Editor: Ana Wraight
Developmental editor: Katharine O'Moore-Klopf
Art director: Stacie Buterbaugh
Marketing: Sheila Boggess
Sales: Wes Lowe
Office coordinator: Melanie Peterson
Graphic interns: Jessica Hollingsworth, Brooke Hernandez & Maricela Fernandez
Indexing: Michelle Graye (indexing@yahoo.com)
Printing production: Data Reproductions
Photography: José Bustamante & Frank Curry

Manufactured in the United States of America

First edition

Publisher's Cataloging-in-Publication
(Provided by Quality Books, Inc.)

Johnson, Darla.
    The art of listening : intuition & improvisation in
    choreography / by Darla Johnson. -- 1st ed.
p. cm.
Includes index.
ISBN-13: 978-1-934302-93-4 (softback)
ISBN-10: 1-934302-93-7 (softback)

1. Improvisation in dance. 2. Choreography.
I. Title.

GV1781.2.J64 2012   792.8
        QBI11-600199

TABLE OF CONTENTS

INTRODUCTION:
WHY THE ART OF LISTENING?

The art of listening … doesn't that sound easy? By now, we already know how to listen, right? I disagree! Listening is quite challenging and demanding. One of the hardest things I do as a choreographer, dancer, and teacher is really listen – to my fellow dancers, to students, to my environment, and especially to myself. As Darla Johnson has eloquently explained in this guide to choreography, listening is exactly where we need to start.

What about the contemporary approach to choreography demands we begin with listening? To begin with, contemporary choreography is deeply rooted in the concept of self-expression. In the early twentieth century, when the first modern dancers declared their independence from the hierarchal ballet establishment, dance, in the Western tradition, was forever changed. These early pioneers created dances inspired by their own experiences, which reflected their emotions, insights, and distinctive perspectives on their world. This commitment to the choreographer's unique artistic voice has become an essential component of contemporary dance – it is what distinguishes it most from other forms of theatrical dance. In contemporary dance, the choreographer's voice is not only what begins the course of dance-making, but it is what we as the audience long to see. Every time I watch a contemporary dance, I look for the ways in which the choreographer's unique vision is being explored.

Modern Dance and its contemporary forms have evolved over time. Due in large part to the grit and determination of many artists before us, the definitions of dance are now much wider. Today, dances take place not just in the theatre, but in shopping malls, on the sides of buildings, in public parks, along downtown streets, and in numerous other site-specific locations. Inclusiveness is also growing in the field as more and more companies embrace dancers of diverse backgrounds – ethnicity, age, body type, and physical ability. The ongoing development of dance is important; it is not a static form. As dancers and choreographers, we must continually reflect and respond to our changing environment; that is, in essence, what makes us contemporary artists.

In order to remain relevant to our wider communities, we as contemporary dancers must let go of narrow and elite definitions of *dance* and *dancer*. By broadening our own vision and collaborating with people different from ourselves, we are also practicing tolerance and acceptance. It is in the diversity of experience where we begin to understand dance as a more expansive concept than we may have previously imagined.

As definitions of *dance* and *dancer* have widened in the contemporary aesthetic, so have the processes for making dances. There certainly is no one right way to construct or create a piece of choreography. For this reason, you should approach this guide with openness and curiosity. You must take risks and work outside of your sense of comfort. How else will you, as an artist, arrive at a new place of reflection or understanding? If, in following this book, you feel irritated, annoyed, or just slightly ahead of where you are comfortable, then great! You are exactly on the right track.

In this guide, Darla Johnson relies on improvisation as a basic tool for choreography. Why? You may have been making dances all of your life without ever thinking about improvisation before. Why must you do it now?

Improvisation is a central beginning place in contemporary dance – the contemporary aesthetic is highly focused on your *unique* voice as choreographer. Through improvisation, you push yourself and try things that are new and often unfamiliar. It is in these unfamiliar, uncomfortable, and unexplored moments where the most interesting material for dance can emerge. As a choreographer, I have learned that, if in the early development of a dance I decide

to let go and not know what the dance may become, I can more rapidly discover new ideas and possibilities for myself as an artist.

Even though there is not one clear way to make a dance, craft is still very important; the process of choreographing is not easy. In fact, making a dance, particularly one that is well crafted and memorable, is very challenging. Choreography takes persistence, tenacity, and hours of hard work. There are important tools explored in this book that any choreographer must learn to understand, manipulate, and use. With these tools in hand, you will learn how to create a dance that communicates your intent as a choreographer with clarity and authenticity.

Darla Johnson's approach, focused on improvisation and intuition, will help guide you through the tricky process of choreography. You must listen first and foremost to your body. By doing this, you will begin a journey of exploration that will help you craft a well-constructed dance. Along your journey, you will be asked to take risks and to try things completely new and different for you as a dancer. This is essential; you should not expect to end up in the same place as you began.

As artists we play highly valuable and significant roles in our communities and culture. One of our most important roles is that of the risk taker. Asking ourselves to push into unexplored territory is vital. We then are able to offer insights, viewpoints, and perspectives that might have been completely missed before. To offer this kind of reflection takes stamina, daring, and a firm belief in the creative process. The opportunity to try something completely new or look at my world in a different way is part of what I enjoy most about my work as a choreographer. Through this, great benefits come to audiences and artists alike. You will ultimately know yourself more clearly and completely. This is perhaps the greatest gift the choreographic journey gives any artist willing to go for the ride.

–Allison Orr

AUTHOR'S NOTE

Who isn't drawn to dance in some way? It's all around us. YouTube, the Internet, and television are all filled with it. It's in the street, on the stage, and in dance clubs everywhere as break dancing, hip hop, country western, salsa, tango, Bollywood, and more. We all move. We all have different rhythms, tempos, and shapes to how we walk and swing our bodies. We're all creating our own unique dance at every moment. The language of dance is all around us.

Watching how the wind blows the trees or birds flock together is also dance. Rain hitting the pavement, butterflies chasing each other, the bulging throat of the anole – rhythm and movement in tandem make up a dance, as well as stillness and breath interspersed with action. I am particularly fond of watching children play. The effortlessness and the variety of moves they make in any given moment can be material for choreography. There is no right way to create a dance. There is only the individual and the will to express oneself. Each choreographer has a process, and exploring and refining the process is the goal.

I started making dances when I was in college. It was exciting and challenging; I wanted to express myself. I believed then, and still believe now, that choreography was the journey toward knowing myself and my place in the world. It's my practice of making choices and using my critical eye and objective self, to get out of my own way and make something better, to dig more deeply into something I want to know more about or gain a deeper understanding of. Intuition and improvisation are the foundation; questioning and objectivity are the tools. Over the years I've made many dances and taught countless others how to make their own.

This book is meant to be a guide, a friend, a small, still voice accompanying you on your journey of creativity and dance-making. Here you will discover a supportive voice that wants you to succeed and is delighted by your ability to tap into your own creativity to make something: to make a dance! Throughout the book, professional choreographers give you advice and guidance for your studies in topics ranging from improvisation to feedback to the final rehearsal process. In addition, you will find case studies from the students of Austin Community College, offering their impression of the exercises and how they benefited.

I hope you find this book useful not only in your choreographic pursuits but also in any other aspect of your life where a creative solution is required or yearned for. Perseverance and play, the willingness to try, and the practice of making choices are all you need to succeed.

–Darla Johnson

1 THE VEHICLE OF CHOREOGRAPHY

"We're fools whether we dance or not, so we might as well dance."

–Japanese proverb

Art Making With the Body

Jumping is a beautiful component of dancing. The sheer joy of elevation and leaving the Earth is an amazing thing, whether you are jumping or watching someone else jump. There are as many ways to start the process of choreographing a dance as you can think of. Jumping into it with the same anticipation you have before a leap is a good energy to bring to the process.

To *choreograph* is a specific and glorious task. When you create with your body, you are the imagination, the tool, and the expression all in one.

In this chapter, you will explore:

- Keeping an artistic journal

- Looking at other artwork

- Recognizing the creative process

Choreography can be described as:

1. The art of symbolically representing dancing

2. The composition and arrangement of dance

This is *art-making* with your body. Instead of using color and material – as in painting and sculpture – you are making art with your torso and limbs, head and feet, neck and shoulders, fingers and toes. You are using your imagination to fuel your physical creative choices. Art-making encompasses the creation of aesthetic form and can be defined as:

1. Skill acquired by experience, study, or observation

2. The conscious use of skill and creative imagination, especially in the production of aesthetic objects

In *contemporary choreography*, you choreograph from your own physical, emotional, and spiritual experience. Contrary to the classical Western form, contemporary choreography focuses less on an existing vocabulary of steps and more on the process of creating a new vocabulary. In addition, contemporary choreography continuously evolves and is reinvented by its creators, defying attempts at a cohesive definition.

Ana Baer Carrillo, Choreographer

Since its conception, modern dance has striven to redefine itself in relation to culture, contemporary life, and the inner condition. As technology has advanced with increasing rapidity since the 1960s, dance makers have found new and often groundbreaking methods for implementing technology into dance. For instance, the hybrid genre video dance, often called dance for camera or dance film, was pioneered in America by filmmakers Maya Deren (in the 1940s) and Shirley Clarke (in the 1950s).

Subsequently, established choreographers, including choreographers Merce Cunningham and Bill T. Jones, made important contributions to the genre. In recent years with the digitalization of the medium, the creation of video dance has become a common practice among choreographers around the globe.

Some of the higher profile modern dance companies producing video work include Rosas (Belgium), Ultima Vez (Brussels), La La La Human Steps, Kaeja d'Dance (Canada), and DV8 Physical Theatre (England) and choreographers Victoria Marks, Cari Ann Shim Sham*, and Marta Renzi.

In 2007, the field of video dance in America experienced a massive enrichment with the creation of the EMPAC DANCE MOViES Commission, launched by the Experimental Media and Performing Arts Center of the Rensselaer Polytechnic Institute. Since then, numerous new and established choreographers have been awarded financial support to create new work.

The genre continues to proliferate rapidly, with the most common venue for the work being niche festivals the world over. Most festivals operate in a similar fashion: an invitation for submission of work, curatorship of the work, and production of one or more screenings of the festival's choices.

Some of the most prolific festivals are:

- Argentina – Festival Video DanzaBa

- Belgium – DANSCAMDANSE

- Brazil – Dança em Foco

- England – Moves

- Greece – MIR festival

- Mexico – agite y sirve

- United States – Dance CameraWest, Dance on Camera Festival, International Screendance Festival, American Dance Festival, San Souci Festival of Dance Cinema, Int'l Dance for the Camera Festival

Headlong Dance Theater, for example, combines a large vocabulary of movement techniques such as ballet, tap, sign language, and Ghanaian folk dance to comment and reflect on subject matters ranging from the 1930s Warsaw Jewish ghetto to Britney Spears. Choreographer Bill T. Jones, along with the Bill T. Jones/Arnie Zane Dance Company, also uses many resources when creating a performance. Jones and the company incorporate visual imagery with music and text to drive a work, such as in the piece *Last Supper at Uncle Tom's Cabin/The Promised Land*, performed in 1990 for the Next Wave Festival at the Brooklyn Academy of Music.

When choreographing, you are accessing your creative ability to identify and deal with a challenge or a set of problems that enlivens the *creative process* and enables you to create a dance that is uniquely yours. Your imagination and physical vitality combine to form a mental image and ignite your creative spark into movement or a series of steps.

Everyone is capable of making creative choices. It is through practice and skill that you become an artist and choreographer. The more questions you can ask yourself about what it is you are doing and trying to express, the more information and material you will be able to gather. You don't have to have the answers to these questions; you just have to be willing to explore them.

Deborah Hay, Choreographer

What if we expand notions of choreography to include the process through which a choreographer transmits a dance to a performer, accounting for the many and often discontinuous threads, visible and invisible, that affect the presence and immediacy of the dancer?

What if dance is how I practice a relationship to my whole body at once as my teacher in relationship to the space in which I am dancing in relationship to time passing in relationship to my audience?

– from *The Other Side of O* by Deborah Hay

Keeping an Artistic Journal

Artists have always kept journals. Artist, inventor, and scientist Leonardo da Vinci kept a journal containing sketches of a large range of topics – from flight to the human body to beautiful buildings, with personal notes throughout. Visual artist Frida Kahlo's journal mixed text with vibrant sketches. Writer, producer, and director Guillermo del Toro even keeps a leather bound sketchbook filled with story ideas and scenes for books and movies.

Your journal is a place to divulge, dream, and envision life and your art. It is the place you go to ask yourself unanswerable questions and to write down ideas and make notes on unusual and beautiful things you see, hear, or do. You can be completely yourself. No one is censoring or judging you when you interact with your journal. You can draw, paint, write poetry, and explore your imagination and feelings.

It is also the place to keep notes on the choreography you are making. You can map out steps and write down or draw the movement you are creating. Choreographers often create their own shorthand to help them remember their choreography.

Jessica Lindberg Coxe, Choreographer

German dance analyst Rudolf von Laban created *Labanotation* to study movement patterns of the human body. Today, Labanotation can be used to document movement, analyze individual movement affinities, aid in dance movement therapy, and inspire creative movement in students of all ages and abilities.

There are various methods for incorporating Labanotation into the choreographic process. The choreographer can notate, or write down, a movement sequence and then look through the notation to see what movement elements are lacking, repeated too often, or require some variation. The system can also be used in collaboration between choreographers when creating a dance, allowing them to build on each other's ideas.

Labanotation can be a useful and creative tool for choreography. You can take the symbols for the basic actions, directions, and pathways and arrange them to create a phrase. Whether you use notation for movement inspiration or for reflection and refinement, it can help you to develop your eye for movement.

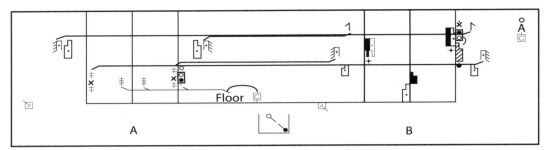

Labanotation of picture on previous page transcribed by Jessica Lindberg Coxe

☑ **LEARN MORE**

Scan the code or visit
http://bit.ly/AoL1lab

▲ Labanotation, which is used for analyzing and recording human movement using symbols, is an example of a standardized system you can use to document the choreography you create. This notation type is used to document human motion, from the position of the arms to the amount of contact the foot should have with the floor.

Exercise 1.1
Starting Your Journal

▶ Find a notebook or journal in a size you like and is portable. You can find unlined drawing journals at any art supply store. Choosing a journal without lines is not necessary, but it will give you the space to make your own drawings. You may even choose to use online journals or digital devices such as the iPad.

▶ Make a list of all the dances you have seen or ones you have already created. For each dance, write down anything you remember that struck you as inventive or left an impression on you. Did you like the energy or the smooth flow of movement in the choreography? Were you emotionally connected to it? Were the costumes particularly striking? Was there a beat or a rhythm that moved you?

▶ Make a list of impressions, do a series of drawings, or write little snippets of impressions of these works.

Exposing Yourself to Other Art Forms

It is important to observe and investigate other art forms. Choreographers have always had deep connections to other art forms and artists. For instance, choreographer Merce Cunningham and visual artist Robert Rauschenberg collaborated for ten years, from 1954-1964. Rauschenberg designed new sets for each performance of Cunningham's *Labyrinthian Dances*, *Rune*, and *Story*, among others, using only materials he collected around the theatre. Throughout the following years, Cunningham used some of Rauschenberg's paintings, including *Immerse* and *Travelogue*, as backdrops for productions.

Exercise 1.2
Exploring Other Art Forms

▶ Have everyone in your group bring in an artistic image from some art form other than dance.

▶ With the members of your group, sit in a circle and listen while each person takes one to two minutes to talk about why he or she chose that particular piece.

▶ After each person's explanation, allow another minute or two for further discussion from the rest of the group. The beauty of this discussion is you will find each person has a unique way of seeing and experiencing art.

Inspiration is not always a formal relationship between artists of various disciplines. Art, music, and dance have had formal and informal working relationships for centuries, continuously inspiring each other. French artist and composer Marcel Duchamp wrote music based on the unpredictability of the 1910s. The ideas created by his pieces inspired John Cage, an experimental composer, to create a score based on amplified household appliance sounds. Inspired by Cage, Christian Marclay created sound collages with turntables used as musical instruments.

Mary Ann Brehm and Lynne McNett, Choreographers

Although art experiences grow out of inherent human need, an art experience can be truly extraordinary, like entering another world. The material of the "art world" is the same as in the everyday world. It is just experienced differently. The art world feels like you are creating it and, at the same time, like it is being created for you and from you. If it is a collaborative effort, the effect is further startling because a new world is being co-created. The art experience requires being fully present in a place where, paradoxically, you are both acting with control and being led by the flow of a situation. Art is about both discovery and creation.

– from *Creative Dance for Learning*: *The Kinesthetic Link*
by Mary Ann Brehm and Lynne McNett

By looking at paintings and photographs, watching plays, viewing video footage of performance art and dance, reading poetry, going to museums and galleries, searching out new music, and attending concerts, you can explore and analyze another artist's process. Doing this also helps you to discover exactly what it is that moves you and excites your sense of artistic adventure.

There is so much art available to you on the Internet alone. You can delve into photography and art sites, poetry forums, video clips on YouTube, and music of all genres. Books on art, architecture, and poetry at your library are fabulous ways to connect with dance and movement. Elements of space and time are present in all art forms and can inspire creative thoughts and actions that lead directly to your own choreography.

Exercise 1.3
Visualizing a Dance

▶ Lie on the floor with your eyes closed and your journal next to you. Imagine a favorite dance you've seen or love to do. You may think of movements that come from sports, children playing, or everyday tasks like sweeping, shoveling, gardening, climbing, and rollerblading. Allow yourself to watch a movie of movements and energy in your mind's eye. Don't try too hard; keep a gentle focus toward opening yourself up to all the movement that is around you all the time.

▶ Choose three movements from these images.

▶ In your mind's eye, place the three movements together into a sequence. None of these moves need to have any connection to each other. They can all be very disparate from each other as far as style and source.

▶ Pick three more movements and add those to the others. Be careful not to censor yourself.

▶ Make a sequence combining the six movements together.

▶ After you've stitched the sequence together, make one change in the order or replace a move with another one. What color comes to mind when you think of this movement sequence? Why did you pick this color? Are there any emotions present? How does it make you feel?

▶ Now transcribe this dance into your journal. You can do it anyway you want. You can draw, color, write free verse, make stick figures, write it as a story or a poem, or use any combination of expressions. It's your unique vision.

Exercise 1.4
Learning to Listen to the Voice of Art

▶ Study a piece of artwork for three minutes, digesting the minute physical details. Really look at all the parts and distinguish the elements from the whole.

▶ Now put aside the artwork and write about what you observed for three minutes in your journal in a stream of consciousness format.

▶ Revisit the artwork for another three minutes, this time paying attention to the emotional and sensory responses you have toward it.

▶ Write in your journal for three minutes about your impressions.

▶ With your classmates or group members, share information and your impressions of the art piece. Be open to all the differences and similarities that appear.

▶ Now, using the two observations, create movement. Allow yourself to investigate and play with what you saw and felt.

▶ Put the movements together and see what your impressions have helped you make. Show them to the class.

Conclusion

Inspiration is everywhere you look. You may hear a piece of music that inspires a dance. You may see an event on the street that inspires a new movement. You may have an emotional exchange with a friend or family member that inspires a theme. Poet Benjamin Zephaniah found inspiration to write political poetry after seeing a poignant picture of a starving Biafran child. Darcey Bussell, principle ballerina of the Royal Ballet, looks for inspiration in the vibrant colors and views of her surroundings. Staying present in your life and noticing what moves you or affects your mood and physical sense of self provides vital information. These elements will drive your creativity into the actual making of a dance.

ACC Student Case Study

Jai Almendarez and Yvonne Keyrouz

One of the studies I found very interesting and useful was Exercise 1.4. For sake of imagery, I used descriptive words that carried depth and color to create a visually responsive world that emulated the painting. During this process, I was taking American Sign Language (ASL) classes and was very captivated by the whole culture. Naturally I was inclined to create a visual atmosphere using ASL. I had an idea to continue with ASL as our means of moving because communicating through an expressive language itself is a fluid way to move.

Once we [Yvonne and I] performed our pieces for each other, we found places where our phrases complemented each other. The difficult part was figuring out what was the message we wanted to convey. It was easiest to take

on personas and have a conversation with each other. Soon it hit us to use the earth, telling its timeless story as our meaning. We found the choreography by using Contact Improvisation to create more phrases and then added signs to those movements. It felt great, as this ASL/Dance was a unique variation in movement.

—Jai

Using Exercise 1.4 as my basis, I wrote down specific details of what was going on in the painting. I built a story based on the emotional response I felt, taking into account the colors of the painting and the expression of the people. I created individual movement using only the details I had written down and linked them together. I then created a phrase based on the emotional aspects of the painting and connected the phrases together, using the first phrase as an introduction to the second bit.

Jai and I began our collaboration by discussing the origins of our phrases and our processes leading up to what we had so far. We had similar beginnings, using the literal details as a basis of movement for an introductory phrase. I loved the idea of incorporating ASL into the movement of the study, and we decided to continue with that idea, folding my phrases into the movement he had already developed.

–Yvonne

Outside Sources

ABSOLUT Fringe Festival in Dublin, Ireland, www.fringefest.com

Guest, Ann Hutchinson, and Tina Curran. *Your Move*. 2nd ed. New York: Routledge, 2007

Ludwig, L.K. *Creative Wildfire: An Introduction to Art Journaling* – Basics and Beyond. Minnesota: Quarry Books, 2010

Rauschenberg, Robert et al. *Robert Rauschenberg: Combines*. London: Steidl, Gerhard Druckerei und Verlag, 2006

The Umbrella Dance Festival in London, United Kingdom, www.danceumbrella.co.uk

Web English Teacher. "Collections of Poetry." Last modified December 31, 2010. www.webenglishteacher.com/poetrycollections.html

Chapter Terms

Art-making: Use of skill, experience, study, observation, and the creative imagination to make a work of art.

Choreographing: Making creative choices with your physical body as the tool for expression and creation.

Contemporary choreography: Choreography made by accessing the physical world as the choreographer knows it.

Creative process: The unique process an artist engages in to create work.

Labanotation: A system that records human movement.

Questions to Consider and Discuss

1. What are the unique qualities that make choreography an art form?

2. What are the elements of creativity and art-making?

3. How do you define an artist's process?

4. What are some different ways keeping a journal can be of use to you?

2 A WARM BODY TO CREATE FROM

"I do not try to dance better than anyone else. I only try to dance better than myself."

–Mikhail Baryshnikov

Readying Your Whole Body

In this chapter, you will explore:

- Focusing on your warm-up

- Warming the spine

- Engaging the core

- Moving the large muscle groups

Being warmed up is an important component of choreographing. You think more clearly with your body when you are warm. The muscles, joints, and bones are harmonizing and ready to fire off your next creative, intuitive movement when you start in a heightened physical state. You also avoid injury; you want to be ready to execute the next movement and not worry about hurting yourself or another dancer.

Being warmed up also helps you focus your attention on the task at hand. Your whole being is ready and alert to work. Your instrument is tuned and ready to take risks and explore new movement. You can be more spontaneous knowing you are warm and ready to create.

Focus on Centering

When you are *centered* and focused on your breath, you can start your warm-up from a calm place. It is important to clear your mind and find a moment of peace, relaxing your body, mind, and spirit and readying yourself to engage in the process of tuning your instrument. Beginning with *passive stretches* helps you to connect with your breath, calms your mind, and allows you to have a deeper, more integrated warm-up.

Exercise 2.1
Centering Yourself

▶ Lie on your stomach on a mat or the floor. Bring your right arm straight out above your head and lay it on the floor, palm down. Fold your left arm on the floor overhead and lay your forehead on your arm. Feel the length of your right side from fingertip to toe. Fold your left knee up, like a bird's wing, next to your side. Try to leave your torso as flat against the floor as possible.

▶ Just stay here and breathe for a minute, focusing on inhalation, exhalation, and the length of your torso.

▶ Now unfold your bent leg from the knee, reaching your foot out and placing it flat on the floor. You're engaging your rotation muscles at the top of the leg as well as activating the arch of your foot. Feel the energy from the top of the leg through your rotation and down around the knee to the outside of the ankle and foot. Try not to tighten your gluteus maximus muscle.

15

▶ Just stay here and breathe for a minute, focusing on the active energy in your extended left leg.

▶ You may now bend your right leg at the knee, taking hold of the foot. You want to reach out from the hip socket as you bend the knee, lengthening through the thighbone, the hamstring, and quadricep muscle.

▶ If you have a hold of your foot, let it go. Start twisting your body to the left, spiraling your spine from the left arm and allowing your head to roll to the left. Let your foot release from the floor, gliding your leg into the spiral. Just lie there, connecting to the spiral in your spine and breath.

▶ Slither back to your front, releasing first the hips then rib cage, shoulders, head, and neck.

▶ Repeat on the other side.

You waste less energy when you are focused fully on your warm-up. You can channel this energy toward the creative process of choreography. All it takes is a little quiet time and attention to tune in to yourself. It all starts with the conscious act of noticing your breath and relaxing your mind.

Listening to Your Muscles and Feeling Your Bones

Lengthening stretches incorporating yoga movements are good ways to get your blood flowing. Activating your spine is essential to being ready to work; it prepares your body to move and to distribute weight and energy to your limbs. It is also important to start mobilizing your joints and warming up your hip flexors and shoulder girdle. This kind of movement releases *synovial fluid* inside the joints and helps to keep them lubricated and healthy.

As you begin to feel yourself from the inside out, you can expand and inhabit yourself more fully. You will become more aware of the needs of your body, both physical and mental, and may notice where you need to spend a little more time inside of yourself.

Peter Kyle, Choreographer

☑ **LEARN MORE**

Scan the code or visit
http://bit.ly/AoL2kyle

Fundamentally, one might say a common goal of most physical training forms is to expand the range of one's movement while also improving one's expressive potential. Slow Tempo provides a simple way for performers of all ages and abilities to address this essential challenge. Developed by Japanese theatre director Shogo Ohta (1939-2007), this approach incorporates a slow movement practice with an improvisational sensibility. In the realm of performance training, it is unique because it invites the individual to move with sensitivity from moment to moment, achieving tremendous delicacy in motion as well as plasticity of the mind. By addressing the incremental shift of weight as the body moves through space, the performer learns to marry thought with kinetic intention and invention with physical articulation. The result is a compelling physical presence. In combination with other modes of dance and theatre training, Slow Tempo provides a platform for exploring the depths of one's concentration in ways seldom afforded in our busy twenty-first century lives. In this place, Ohta believed "we find fresh expression to defamiliarize our daily experience – to look again."

Exercise 2.2
Creating a Warm Spine

▶ Kneel on a mat or the floor with your knees directly under your hips and your wrists directly under your shoulders. Splay your fingers out and keep contact with your fingertips to the floor.

▶ Inhale and lift your head and your tailbone together, arching your back.

▶ Exhale and drop the head and tail, scooping your belly into the spine and curving your back.

▶ Inhale to arch, exhale to curve. Perform the sequence five or six times.

▶ Now tuck your toes and lift your hips up into the air and stretch back through your wrists, arms, and shoulders. Lengthen your spine, keeping your *wing tips* and shoulders down. Try to reach your heels back into the floor. Breathe deep breaths and think of lengthening through your whole body from head to heels.

▶ Come to the balls of your feet and lift your belly into your spine, lowering your knees to the floor. Sit back on your heels and rest.

▶ Return to your hands and knees, lifting your tail back and pressing backward into the position once again.

▶ Lift the right leg up behind you, keeping your pelvis horizontal to the floor. Press back through the shoulders and heels of your hands.

▶ Exhale and press back again, this time opening the whole right side of your body and looking under your right arm. Stretch from fingertips to toes, reaching the leg and extending through your hip socket.

▶ Reach the toe higher and then behind you, bending the knee and stretching across the hip.

▶ Bring the leg down and lower yourself again, sitting on your heels and resting.

▶ Come back up and repeat on the other side

Core Movement

Activating your abdominal muscles is an important factor in your warm-up. Your *core* is the center of your body, where all movement emanates from. *Pilates* work done on a mat or the floor is a common way for dancers to get this muscle group engaged. Creating a strong core connection allows you to have a fuller range of movement. It is what stabilizes and supports you as you move fully through space.

Exercise 2.3
Activating Core Movement

▶ Lie on your back with your feet on the floor and your knees pointing to the ceiling in a neutral pelvis position. Your arms are at your side with your palms down. Make sure you are not tucking or tilting your pelvis; lie relaxed with a natural curve to your lower back. Inhale deeply into the back of the lungs, pressing your back into the floor. Exhale, pushing air out through the mouth, and engage your deep lower abdominal muscles without moving your pelvis.

▶ Put pressure into your feet and lift your pelvis one vertebra at a time until your core is in line with your ribcage. Do not press the pelvis higher than your ribs. Stay in position and take a deep breath.

Exhale, engage the lower abdominal muscles, and then sequentially roll down, one vertebra at a time, to the neutral pelvis position. Do this three to four more times. Try to engage the inner thigh muscles as you put pressure through your feet to lift the pelvis up and then release it back down to neutral position. Focus on smooth, even movements while rolling up and down the spine.

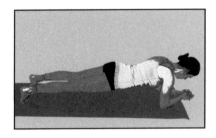

▶ Continuing in the neutral pelvis position, roll your pelvis up as previously described and stay in position. Inhale. Exhale, pushing the air out. Engage the lower abdominals, release your sternum, and lift the right leg up with your knee bent at a right angle. Inhale while lowering the right leg. Exhale. Scoop your belly and lift the left leg at the knee at a right angle. Inhale and lower your knee. Repeat eight sets.

▶ Roll over onto your stomach and lace your fingers together, opening your elbows directly below your shoulders. You are going to do a modified plank position, which will activate all of the muscles in your core. Keep your shoulders down and relaxed, not up by your ears. Reach your legs out behind you and rest on the balls of your feet. Lift your body off of the floor, creating a nice, flat tabletop with your body. Do not tuck or tilt the pelvis, but engage your abdominals to maintain a straight line. Breathe deeply and try to keep the position for one minute. Release slowly and sit back on your heels and rest.

Taking the time to investigate for yourself how your core supports you is necessary to having a strong technique and stable *alignment*. A strong center requires an ongoing relationship with yourself. Your body is constantly changing and each day is a new opportunity for you to pay attention and explore and connect. It is the connections inside of you that radiate outward and make you a strong dancer.

Large Muscle Groups

Finally, to complete your warm-up, focus on the large muscle groups in your legs, hips, and arms. These locomotion muscles help to propel you through space as you run, leap, and twirl. They also build your cardiovascular strength and endurance to keep you dancing for extended periods of time.

Exercise 2.4
Activating the Large Muscle Groups

▶ Take a walk around the room, releasing your weight through the pelvis. Feel the energy from your feet connecting to the floor. Let your arms swing loosely at your sides. Stop anywhere in the room and bring your legs underneath your hips in a parallel position, toes pointing forward.

▶ Release your knees. Raise your arms up to the side with your fingertips reaching out directly from your shoulders. Inhale. Press through the feet and inner thigh muscles, lowering the arms and lengthening the legs to a straight position. Be careful to not push your knees back, locking them into a hyper-extended position. Let your head be loose and floating on the spine. Repeat ten times.

▶ Take a short jog around the room. Find a new place and stop.

▶ Inhale. Lengthen and engage your belly, feeling energy up through your spine. Rock back on the heels and open up your feet, leaving your arms relaxed at your side. Try to keep your body in one long, engaged line.

▶ Inhale. Lift the toes and bring the legs back to parallel. Repeat five times. On the fifth repetition, bring your heels together as much as possible without forcing

your feet open more than the rotation you have in your hips.

▶ From this position inhale deeply and then exhale, releasing into a plié. Raise your arms up in front of your body to the bottom of your ribcage, keeping your elbows lifted and arms rounded. Make sure to keep your knees over the center of the feet and your pelvis released under the ribcage. Repeat ten times.

▶ Take another jog around the room at a faster pace. Find a new place in the room to work.

▶ Then rotate the legs, opening them wider than the hips into a second position. Inhale. Exhale, releasing your legs into a plié, raising the arms up into a *V* position, reaching your fingertips out. Exhale. Lower your arms while straightening the legs, keeping the pelvis directly under the ribcage. Make sure your knees are over the center of the feet. Repeat ten times.

▶ In parallel position, move through the space, *prancing* briskly. Roll through your feet, toes, balls of your feet, and heels to warm up your feet and ankles. Make sure your heels release into the floor with each prance. Arms are hanging loosely at your sides.

▶ In a rotated position, step with your right leg, swinging the left leg up to *attitude* with your right arm in first position at the bottom of the ribcage. Step and switch, while moving through the space.

You also need these large muscles to sustain strong balances for *adagio* work. When these muscles are warm, you can access their strength more readily and hold your balance for longer in a steadier stance.

Exercise 2.5
Creating Your Own Warm-Up

▶ The previous exercises are all examples of how to get your body and mind ready to create your own dances. Using these as your template, create a warm-up where you have two or three exercises focusing on each of the main areas of the body – spine, core, and large muscle group. Feel free to use any of the exercises listed previously as part of your plan, but the idea here is to customize your own plan.

▶ Look at each of the categories in Exercises 2.1-2.4 and investigate websites, books, and DVDs for other exercises or movements to target the same muscle groups. Devise a warm-up based on your research. More than likely, there is one or more area where you will want or need to expand. Listen to your body.

▶ Another option would be to investigate other dance or movement forms such as African dance, hip hop, tai chi, yoga, Pilates, butoh, or Slow Tempo dance. Some of these may be available on DVD, online, or through local classes. Challenging yourself to move in different ways builds knowledge of how your body works and moves, which gives you new movement ideas to introduce into your own choreographic style.

Conclusion

Warming up is an important step when creating or performing a dance. It prepares the body and mind, centering them to work together and to focus on the task at hand. You will become more aware of your body through lengthening stretches, such as yoga poses. Activating your core will help you to stabilize and gives you more range of movement. Strengthening the large muscle groups will help make your movements more powerful, allowing you to propel through space. A good warm-up routine is pivotal to your choreographing process.

Trevor Revis

The warm-up is essential for my process as a choreographer and dancer. It allows me to center myself, activate my body, and put myself into a creator/dancer mode. I find when I take the time to fully stretch my body and strengthen my arms, legs, and core, I can fully perform all of the leaps, lifts, and spins I love to do. When I don't fully stretch beforehand, accidents seem to occur. I'm slowly beginning to understand I'm not as durable as I was when I was younger, when I could do all sorts of crazy moves without sitting down to stretch. Now when I try to perform a windmill or a huge leap without warming up, my body tends to punish me for it.

I have also found when I'm dancing with a group, warming up together first is best. It allows the group to share their breathing and their movement and slowly become attuned to each other, which creates a shared sense of community. This is essential when dancers are moving together because if all the wild jumps and crazy lifts are going to be shared in one space, trust is going to be needed. I believe a sense of community helps create the necessary trust.

I have also found a warm-up once or twice a day has created significant changes to my physique. Simple strengthening moves – like the plank, sit ups, and hamstring/leg exercises done alongside stretches such as downward dog, lunges, and the straddle – have improved my physique incredibly and have kept me flexible and strong enough to dance full out every time I rehearse.

Outside Sources

☑ **LEARN MORE**

Scan the code or visit
http://bit.ly/AoL2st-j

Staugaard-Jones, Jo Ann. *The Anatomy of Exercise and Movement: For the Study of Dance, Pilates, Sport and Yoga*. Sussex: Lotus Publishing, 2010

Gates, Rolf and Katrina Kenison. *Meditations from the Mat: Daily Reflections on the Path of Yoga*. New York: Anchor, 2002

Hammond, Sandra Noll. *Ballet Basics*. Illinois: Waveland Press, Inc., 2011

Franklin, Eric. *Conditioning for Dance*. Illinois: Human Kinetics, 2003

Friedman, Philip and Gail Eisen. *The Pilates Method of Physical and Mental Conditioning*. New York: Penguin, 2004

Hackney, P. *Making Connections: Total Body Integration Through Bartenieff Fundamentals*. New York: Routledge, 2000

Watkins, Andrea. *Dancing Longer, Dancing Stronger: A Dancer's Guide to Improving Technique and Preventing Injury*. Hightstown, NJ: Princeton Book Company, 1994

Chapter Terms

Adagio: Slow, sustained movement.

Alignment: The placement of your bones in relationship to moving and dancing.

Attitude: A dance position where the leg is lifted to hip level with the leg bent at a 90 degree angle and the calf is horizontal and parallel to the floor.

Centered: Focused, calm, and ready to work.

Core: Your body's center, where movement and breath connect and emanate from.

Lengthening stretches: Stretches to elongate the muscles and get your blood flowing.

Neutral pelvis: Not tucking or tilting your pelvis, but lying relaxed with a natural curve to your lower back.

Passive stretches: Stretches to relax you and help you to get in touch with yourself.

Pilates: A core-strengthening method created by Joseph Pilates.

Prancing: Moving through space with toes, balls of feet, heels, and knees lifting with a slight suspension in each step.

Synovial fluid: Lubricating fluid released inside the joints.

Wing tips: The bottom points of the scapula.

Questions to Consider and Discuss

1. What is centering?

2. How does centering help the warm-up process?

3. What is the importance of a good warm-up in choreography?

4. What is the importance of your core muscles?

5. What can you do to strengthen your alignment?

3 INTUITION

"Dancing is just discovery, discovery, discovery."

–*Martha Graham*

Learning to Listen to the Creative Voice

Intuition is the voice, the tool, and the inner guide that will lead you in the process and craft of choreography. What is intuition? Intuition can be defined as:

1. Quick and ready insight

2. Immediate apprehension or cognition; the power or faculty of attaining direct knowledge or cognition without rational thought and inference

In this chapter, you will explore:

- Listening to your inner voice

- Letting go of judgment

- Making choices

Intuition is the voice inside that speaks to you when you are making decisions. It is the voice you hear when you are not quite sure where you are going, but something tells you to turn at the next corner. It is how you just know something. Artists engage their intuition all of the time. Your inner guide helps you along the path of discovering exactly what it is you want to say or write or draw or paint or choreograph.

Trusting Ourselves

It is vital to trust yourself. Trusting in yourself is believing you, like all people, have something worthwhile to say. It is believing that creative expression, no matter what the form, is open to all people and is a necessary part of life. You have to know in your heart that you are a creative being and you have something to express. You do not censor or stifle that knowledge. Intuition is free to work when you are open to the creative process and when you are open to exploring.

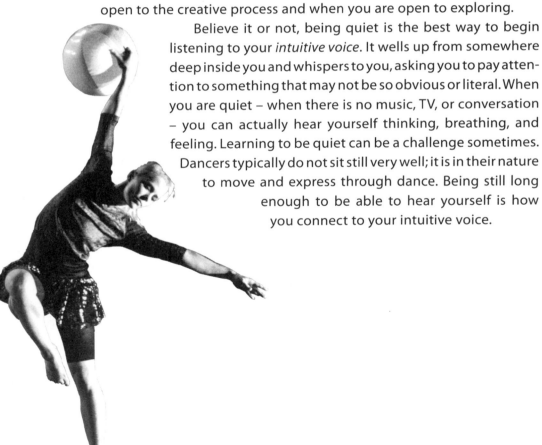

Believe it or not, being quiet is the best way to begin listening to your *intuitive voice*. It wells up from somewhere deep inside you and whispers to you, asking you to pay attention to something that may not be so obvious or literal. When you are quiet – when there is no music, TV, or conversation – you can actually hear yourself thinking, breathing, and feeling. Learning to be quiet can be a challenge sometimes. Dancers typically do not sit still very well; it is in their nature to move and express through dance. Being still long enough to be able to hear yourself is how you connect to your intuitive voice.

Exercise 3.1
Sitting Still

▶ Wander around the studio, really looking at the space. Begin noticing the cor-
ners, the door, the windows, and all the
details of the studio. Find a spot you
gravitate toward and sit down. Get
comfortable.

▶ Breathe. Notice your breath and just sit still. Let your mind wander, but mostly
just pay attention to your breathing. There is no right or wrong way to do this.
You are just sitting and being quiet and noticing your breath and the thoughts
that arise.

▶ Try to not get attached to any sequence of thoughts. Just let the thoughts
come and go. You are just being quiet and practicing listening for your intuitive
voice to appear. See if you can sit still for five minutes without fidgeting.

In choreography, your whole being is involved in making dances,
and listening to your body is a way of becoming conscious. There is
no separation of body, mind, and spirit in the creative process. It is
important to open our physical selves up in order to hear the movement more clearly. You need to be able to listen through your muscles and bones; you need to have *body consciousness*. This means
you are aware of what you are doing and of the physical choices you
are making. To do this at a higher level of consciousness, you need
to learn to be still and to listen to your body as well as be warmed
up. It is like being quiet to listen and hear; you also have to be physically warm to access your *movement voice* (see Chapter Two, "A Warm
Body to Create From"). Your movement voice is where your dance
comes from. It is the tool you express yourself with. Learning to be
still long enough to be able to hear yourself, though, is how you connect to your intuitive voice.

No Judgment

The intuitive voice has no time for judgment. When you start to judge what you are hearing and experiencing, you shut down your deeper thoughts and intuitions, which cuts off the creative flow. You have to say "yes" and just listen with your being (see Chapter Four, "Improvisation and the Unique Voice"). You cannot judge your intuitive and movement voices; you just have to listen and move.

A *defeatist voice* is a voice that says you have no good or original ideas. It claims you are not creative, smart, or talented and you have no potential to choreograph a dance. The defeatist voice says you are not capable of coming up with a *concept* for a dance and following the concept through; it tells you that you have nothing to express. This is just not true (see Chapter Eight, "Theme").

You have to silence the defeatist voice; you have to get out of your own way. Think back to past successes, when the movements you created or performed flowed perfectly. Remember the feeling of triumph and hold onto it. You can also write out daily affirmations to remind yourself of what you want to accomplish and increase your positive energy, shutting out the inner critic. If you just start working, moving, and listening, something creative will happen. You learn by paying attention with your whole self. The key is to create time and space to do it in and then to get going.

Once you start working, listening, and exploring, there is energy at play. You want to keep saying "yes" to the energy, hang onto it, and follow

it through. You want to follow the *movement thread*, which is like a string of little pearls that make up a strand of a necklace. Each little movement leads to the next, and you just keep adding on. Go with it. Let the movement lead you. Do not let your defeatist voice and nagging judgments into the conversation. By listening with your body and staying open to the *next right movement*, you allow your intuitive voice to be heard. The flow of creativity enables you to create movement thread after movement thread, which then allows you to start sensing the next right movement. That is how a dance is made.

Andrew Long, Choreographer

Our bodies are fully engaged in the expression of dance but often left out of the creation of it. How ironic that, as dance makers, we give so much "thought" to the choreographic process. What if your creative studio experience happened suddenly and unexpectedly, without the involvement of conscious thought or analysis?

One of the greatest gifts a dance maker can explore is the process of not knowing. Let the wisdom of your body lead you. Your whole body is made up of trillions of cells, all interlinked and functioning as a whole system. Shifting from mind-thinking creativity to body-awareness creativity is paramount to breaking through and fully expressing your art. Engaging your whole body as a creative navigation system will assist this breakthrough. Let your body's intuitive impulses surface to create the dance. The result will be one of surprise and delight.

We tend to let our mind get in the way, and our internal chatter machine preempts our natural impulses. We get into the habit of routine thought, focusing on what others have said or will say. We let outside convention dictate the way things are supposed to be.

Be willing to let go of expectation, your attachment to outcome, and ego based on what others might say or think. Letting others dictate the outcome will only result in mediocrity. What would happen if you censored your censor and let your full body engage as a source of creativity? Your creative expression can only be revealed through your uniqueness, which intrinsically originates from your willingness to let your unparalleled brilliance shine through. (It is already there, so let it shine.)

Develop a studio practice that begins with you being fully you. Present your whole body as a creative source. It is a commitment to trusting your own vast and infinite knowledge and abilities instead of choreographing from your head. From this place of expansion, you'll discover a whole new creative world.

☑ **LEARN MORE**

Scan the code or visit
http://bit.ly/AoL3anl

Making Choices

Once you are able to follow the movement thread, you want to start paying attention to the choices you are making. Some movements and dance steps are familiar and comfortable. They are the ones you have learned, repeated, and enjoyed performing (see Chapter Four, "Improvisation and the Unique Voice"). All of these are good movements, but what you are attempting to do here is to find new ways of moving and dancing. You want to find movements that are authentic to you and your way of physically expressing yourself but are not necessarily within your comfort zone.

Now your rational mind can begin to kick into gear and start to observe the choices you are making. Are you continually choosing the same movements? Are there ways to change the movement and make it more your own? Of course there are. At this point in the process, you can aim to recognize when you are repeating movements and begin to change them from the start. Maybe in mid-step you discern you are about to repeat the same old leap to the side, so you turn it around in midair and bend your leg where you would have otherwise extended it. Your body consciousness is kicking in, and you are allowing your intuitive voice to express some options.

It is all about getting busy. Talking does not make a dance; doing makes a dance. There will be plenty of time later to make notes, dream, and listen to music; there will be time to record the dance. When you are physically engaged in the process of choreographing, then you can begin *sensing the dance*. You allow the dance to speak to you and have its own life. Something starts to resonate and energy begins to build, and you just keep working. What you are trying to express is enlivened by the mere attention and focus you are giving to the idea. You start listening for prompts your intuitive voice is giving, and you *follow the process*. This is all part of the same idea, the same way of approaching the choreographic process. You move, listen, engage your senses, and pay attention to your movements as you attend to your intuitive voice. To follow the process takes practice just like everything in dance.

Exercise 3.2

Following the Process: Figure Eights

▶ Start with your hand, circling your wrist and making figure eights. Explore the different ways you can move your wrist and fingers in a figure eight.

▶ Move the figure eight to your elbows, exploring the shape with them. Do not think about it; just focus on the idea of the shape.

▶ Now move the shape to your shoulder and then your whole arm. Repeat with the other arm. There is no right way or wrong way of doing this. You are just exploring, listening to your body rhythm, and following the movement thread.

▶ Do the same thing with your leg, starting at the ankle and working up to the hip socket.

▶ Make figure eights with your hips and your spine.

▶ Choose five figure eight movements from various parts of this exercise.

▶ Find a partner and collaborate to put both of your movements together so you each have a total of ten moves. Look for alternative ways of sequencing the movements so you both are not doing the same thing. Perform them together as a duet.

Conclusion

You are most likely not going to create your masterpiece on the first try. However, you will learn something about yourself and your intuitive and movement voices and how to follow a movement thread. Making dances is a process. Each time you make one will be different yet somewhat similar. If you are truly paying attention, you will learn something new about the choreographic process each time. You will start to become braver about trying different ideas and more eager to listen to your intuitive voice. You will trust the crazy notions that pop into your head and the voice that guides you through the creation of the dance. You will start looking for new ways to construct and deconstruct materials. You will enliven the dance space with energy and subtext and will surprise yourself again and again.

ACC Student Case Study

Tara Baker

Intuition is something that is cogent and vital for natural movement. When you think too hard about what will be next, you tend to lose the energy for creating the piece. Something that really helped me with the figure eight exercise was taking simple, pedestrian gestures from everyday activities and turning them into abstract movements. This is a brilliant idea because you can continue to do the same gesture, making it larger and more acute with intention each time it is executed. No one will ever be able to tell you were only brushing your teeth or throwing a baseball.

After the initial movements, we were partnered with someone. My partner and I watched the choreography we had created based on these gestures, and then we pasted our phrases together. In the beginning of our piece, we danced our own choreography and found places where we could meet, a spot where we could become one. When this moment was found, we meshed our choreography together, adding lifts and transitions to mix and match our gestures. Both of us have our own unique way of dancing and it was nice to learn and exchange styles. Another fascinating part of this, something I still think about today, was a moment when our palms were out; he was giving and I was receiving the energy. Other students noticed this, and it really connected us during this process. The figure eight process has been the best choreographic experience of my life so far. I not only created a beautiful piece, but I made a lifelong friend.

Outside Sources

Osho. *Meditation: The First and Last Freedom*. New York: St. Martin's Griffin, 2004

Vaughan, Frances E. *Awakening Intuition*. New York: Anchor, 1978

☑ **LEARN MORE**

Scan the code or visit
http://bit.ly/AoL3jc

Moore, Thomas. *Care of the Soul: A Guide for Cultivating Depth and Sacredness in Everyday Life*. New York: Harper Perennial, 1994

Cameron, Julia. *The Artist's Way*. New York: Tarcher, 2002

Chapter Terms

Body consciousness: Being observant of your physical self, habits, and the choices you make.

Concept: An idea or theme behind and underneath a dance.

Defeatist voice: The negative internal voice telling you that you are not a choreographer, artist, or someone who can make creative choices.

Follow the process: Following your intuitive voice through the process of creating a dance.

Intuition: Your inner guide to making creative choices.

Intuitive voice: The quiet, still voice guiding you on the choreographic path.

Movement thread: Little pieces of movement strung together.

Movement voice: Your unique movement choices.

Next right movement: Listening to your intuitive voice and allowing your movement choices to flow.

Sensing the dance: Ability to hear the dance you are working on and let it guide you in the process.

Questions to Consider and Discuss

1. What is intuition?

2. What processes can help you to better listen to your intuition?

3. How does judgment hold you back?

4. What can you do to help yourself continually make movement choices?

5. What are some words or phrases of encouragement you can write down or say to yourself about listening to your intuitive voice?

6. What did you learn from Exercise 3.2?

4 IMPROVISATION AND THE UNIQUE VOICE

"To be fully alive, fully human, and completely awake is to be continually thrown out of the nest."

–Pema Chödrön

What Is Improvisation?

Improvisation is the basis of all creativity. Somewhere inside each of us is an intuitive voice that thrives on expressing itself. Each day you access the voice, consciously or unconsciously, to make spontaneous decisions. Whether it's in the clothes you're choosing to wear or the lunch you're planning to have, you make an informed and improvised choice at each moment based on your intuitive voice.

In this chapter, you will explore:

- Learning to improvise

- Incorporating muscle memory

- Using space and shape to make movement

Dance improvisation is the same thing. To improvise can be described as:

1. To compose, play, dance, or sing extemporaneously

2. To make, invent, or arrange offhand

3. To make or fabricate out of what is conveniently on hand

Dancers often are afraid to move outside of the comfort zone of the style, technique, or type of training where they have experience. *Muscle memory* is a powerful force. Pay attention to the way you brush your teeth, put on your socks, or wash a dish. Most of us stand and perform these everyday movements in the exact same way. These are our movement habits. Dance often happens in this way, too. We get comfortable in how we move. It feels good and looks good to us. We feel safe and confident in what we're doing. Often what we're doing, however, is repeating and executing dance vocabulary someone else showed us.

In order to take a risk, in order to break free of these patterns, you have to be willing to feel uncomfortable. You have to be willing to feel a bit out of control, like you're twirling on the edge of the universe, because that is what you're doing in dance improvisation. You're riding the edge of what you know and looking for new ways to express yourself.

The first thing you have to remember when improvising is you can't make a mistake. You can only keep exploring and making continuous choices about what is at hand. There is no wrong way to improvise; there is only the continual practice of *making choices*. Remember, you do this every day in some way or another. It's being fearless more than anything else. Not being afraid to look or feel silly, not look beautiful, not feel strong, or to not be in control.

Nina Martin, Choreographer

Improvisation is a recognized aspect of modern dance training. As an area of study, it is used in much of modern dance training as a way for students to become uninhibited with their movements and as a tool for developing their pre-planned choreography. Presently, dance improvisation as a performance practice is of great interest to many postmodern dance artists and theorists, and it is my area of research as well. Improvisational dance can be broken down into three distinct forms: the Solo Body, the Coupled Body, and the Ensemble Body with the ideal improviser accomplished in all three.

For my own practice, I use *ReWire: Dancing States* (improvisation as a dance technique), *Contact Improvisation* (improvisation as a duet form), and *Ensemble Thinking* (strategies for group improvisation), to hone these areas of improvisation. Each of these forms requires a different skill set and, when mastered, represents a substantial body of knowledge from which to create dance. As you gain more experience, you will begin to sense, while working on a dance, when a highly deliberated structure or a more spontaneous approach best supports your creative goals.

Using Improvisation to Become Uninhibited: Learning how to move freely in your body without judgment is a wonderful feeling. However, after years of mimicking a teacher's movement and having your own movement analyzed and judged by teachers, it may be difficult to "let go" and experience dancing without "the little voice" in your head uselessly commenting on the value of your efforts. Many artists have developed scores to circumvent the "the little voice" and allow you to focus on a compositional task. I use the *Fussy Baby Dance* and the *Neuro Dance* from *ReWire: Dancing States* to circumvent judgment. Choreographer Trisha Brown's score for her work *Locus* (1975) is another good example of a compositional task that refocuses your mind away from judgment and toward composition/choreography. Becoming uninhibited in your movement is only the first step. The next step is to spontaneously choreograph your improvising body.

Using Improvisation to Create Pre-Planned Choreography: Many choreographers make video recordings of their improvisations and then re-learn interesting sections from the monitor. This can be a very useful tool because the movement generated through improvisation is often more complex and idiosyncratic than movement created while also trying to remember it.

☑ **LEARN MORE**

Scan the code or visit
http://bit.ly/AoL4nina

Using Improvisation to Create Choreography in Performance: Some dance artists specialize in improvisational dance in performance. To do this well, the artist must be well-practiced in creating dance compositions in "real time" since there is not time to contemplate one's choices during performance. This requires the artist to be sensitive to emerging compositions in order to build on and extend these ideas through time. Composition exercises such as *One Idea* from *Ensemble Thinking* begin to extend one's awareness beyond oneself to include the ensemble.

The next thing to remember is everyone is creative. It is part of being a human. It just requires opening our hearts and minds to the essence of creativity. The essence of creativity is not saying "no" to anything but saying "yes" to everything. There is no flow in *no*; it stops energy. *Yes* expands energy and allows room for new ideas to come forth by requiring you to get out of your own way. You have to leave the nagging, judgmental voice outside of the studio door and be present to the moment. You must breathe and stay connected to yourself, feeling yourself and knowing you have something to say, something to move and dance about. Ultimately, it's about saying "yes" to yourself and allowing your own unique, creative voice to have expression. Remember, it's about being fearless, not self-conscious and doing it for yourself, not others. Say "yes" to yourself. Don't be afraid to be seen by others and don't be afraid to look at yourself and to see something new and different.

It's also about surprising yourself! How fun is that? Think of times when you see something, a particular dance or dance move, and you say, "Wow!" Look for those moments in your own movement, your own exploration. Surprise yourself again and again and make this the normal response to your improvisations.

Everyone has a unique physical language and style, and everyone begins with a unique foundation. Just like there are no two snowflakes alike, there are no two human beings alike. In improvisation, especially in relationship to choreography, we are looking to expand what we already know, to build and express something true to our own movement voice so we can create a dance that is simply ours. Keep listening to your own voice and remember trying is accomplishing something. Moving and exploring are the key components of improvisational dance. Being present with yourself and your surroundings and saying "yes" are essential.

Learning to Improvise

When learning to improvise, you must cultivate your ability to *focus*. To focus means to be attentive to what you're doing, to keep your energy and attention on the task at hand, and to keep dancing, exploring, and allowing the creative juices to flow. You have to stop your mind from stepping in and distracting you from expression; you have to ignore your insecurities or those of someone else's. Focus requires you say "yes" to whatever it is you're doing and know you are doing the right thing at the right time and staying present.

One particularly good way to practice your focus is to breathe. When you are conscious of your breathing, you are connected to yourself. You relax and can be more present with yourself, your body, and your being. The next time you're driving a car or riding your bicycle or standing at a busy intersection, notice your breath. Notice if you are fully exhaling or holding tension. Practice on becoming focused and aware of your breath (see Chapter Two, "A Warm Body to Create From").

Another important aspect of improvisation is being able to follow something through to its natural end. Listen and keep making choices; don't let your judgmental voice near the improvisation you're working on. Explore and follow the movements until you feel like your improvisation is done. This should be fun; call it *riding the groove* and enjoy it. Allow yourself to be playful. It's a gift to enjoy and perpetuate.

Improvisation is also a way to understand your own movement vocabulary. As you begin to investigate concepts and structures, you will also begin to notice your own movement patterns and *stock moves*. Stock moves are the ones you find yourself doing repeatedly; you probably learned them in one of your favorite teacher's classes. They feel good. You feel strong and beautiful when you do them. These are not bad or wrong movements. They just do not push you to discover your own movement vocabulary.

Exercise 4.1
Exploring Your Movement

▶ Take a couple of your favorite stock moves – jumps, slides, turns, or extensions, for instance. Explore doing the moves backwards or upside down, twisting them or letting them fall to the floor. Manipulate the movements you love into something else entirely, making them your own.

Your unique movement vocabulary is your voice, your style, and your way of expressing something from your deep self. It's important to cultivate this tool because it's the way to make an authentic dance that speaks from your own artistic self. It's how choreographers Martha Graham, Merce Cunningham, and Katherine Dunham all did it.

Muscle Memory

Muscle memory is what we use to remember steps and choreography. It is the integration of our brains and our bodies, allowing us to remember movement and movement patterns. This is an essential tool for developing choreography through improvisation. It's important to hone this ability. Repeat the move a number of times until you feel like your muscle memory has kicked in. This is how you can start to expand your own movement vocabulary.

Exercise 4.2
Exploring Your Inspiration

▶ Choose a piece of music you're inspired by or a theme you want to express.

▶ Set up a video camera and forget it's there. It's important to not try to impress yourself with all the fabulous dance moves you know. Stay true to your intention to explore and discover new movement that could become part of a dance.

▶ As you watch the video, you can decide what movements or series of movements fit into your dance.

▶ Make notes in your journal about these movements.

If you do not wish to pause in your creative process to develop your muscle memory, a video camera can help you to see your own movement and repeat it later on. Many choreographers set up a video camera and improvise in front of it. You can then relearn your movements at another time.

Beginning Improvisation

Improvisation is a way into a dance, a way to start doodling. Visual artists and architects make initial drawings and sketches. Choreographers make movement and pieces of dance to look at, think about, and develop into something whole and cohesive.

Exploring Body Parts

A good way to start thinking with your body is to explore different body parts and how they move. It's a very simple process and is full of information and fun. It also helps to warm you up and to get your creative juices flowing.

Exercise 4.3
Investigating Your Range of Movement

▶ Start with your head and neck. Think loose and free. Isolate the movement so it is all above the shoulders. Investigate all the different ways you can move your head on the top of your spine. Use different rhythms; move smooth or jerky. Go as slow as you possibly can. How many ways can you find to rotate and undulate your head and neck?

▶ Now do the same thing with your shoulders. Investigate the range of movement you have in your shoulder girdle and scapula. Isolate the right side from the left side and see if you notice any differences from side to side.

► Next use both of your arms. Swing them, circle them, and propel them behind you, in front of you, and all around you. Explore the different sections of the arms, from finger joints to wrist, wrist to elbow, elbow to shoulder.

► Now isolate your ribcage. Move it side to side in a lateral movement. Fan the fingers of the ribs open by stretching up and down. Twist and move one side, forward and back, and then the other side. Explore and see how many different ways you can move your ribcage.

► Hips are fun: circling and tilting, dropping and thrusting. Move your hips in as many ways as you can.

► The spine is incredibly flexible and expressive. Find as many ways as possible to engage it.

► Don't forget the legs and the feet. You get the idea now. Isolate these different body parts and learn to explore them in ways that are not part of any vocabulary you know. All of this exploration will be helpful when you are trying to find the right movement to express yourself in your choreography.

Creating Shape

Creating shape is one of the essential components of defining your own unique choreographic vocabulary. In ballet, classical Indian dance, flamenco, Native American, and other dance forms there are very recognizable shapes and positions. In contemporary dance, we are looking to express our own voice and create our own shapes and steps. The shapes we choose help us to define our vocabulary. We're still creating from the foundation of our training and experience, but we are using that foundation as a springboard into our own choreographic voice.

Exercise 4.4
Creating Shape

▶ There is a difference between exploring a body part and making shape with a body part. Find a piece of music without lyrics. With your arms, make different shapes to the beat of the music. Keep changing the shape of your arms and look for new forms of articulation.

▶ Do the same thing with your spine and torso.

▶ Do the same thing with your legs.

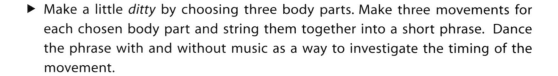

▶ Now start over, following the same sequence of the arms, the spine and torso, and the legs, but do it without music, really taking your time to feel all of the different shapes. Move slowly from one shape to the next, articulating each part.

▶ Make a little *ditty* by choosing three body parts. Make three movements for each chosen body part and string them together into a short phrase. Dance the phrase with and without music as a way to investigate the timing of the movement.

While we are looking at shape, we want to become aware of the use of symmetrical and asymmetrical shape. *Symmetry* creates a balanced, even look. When you create a symmetrical shape, both sides of the plumb line, or the spine, mirror each other so each side is making the same shape. The energy of a symmetrical shape is strong and focused. Think of cheerleading and drill teams. *Asymmetry* typically has more flow, is more fluid, and makes the eye travel around the shape more. Asymmetrical shape is when both sides of the spine are different. The energy tends to be kinetic and off balance. Think *capoeira* and *Contact Improvisation*.

Exercise 4.5
Exploring Symmetry and Asymmetry

▶ Have a partner clap out an even rhythm for you. Stand in place and make one symmetrical shape after another to the beat, trying to never repeat yourself. Go slow and stay focused on simple changes and progressions. Trade places with your partner and let them make the shapes.

▶ Repeat the exercise. This time explore asymmetrical shape with your partner clapping and you changing shape. Trade places again.

▶ This last time, go back and forth between symmetry and asymmetry, changing from one to the other with each beat.

▶ Choose four symmetrical shapes and four asymmetrical shapes. Put them together into a phrase in any order as long as you include all eight shapes.

▶ Share these phrases with the class or with other dancers.

Pedestrian Movement

Dancers often walk, hop, skip, stand in place, and run in dances. This is called *pedestrian movement*. Pedestrian movement says something very simple and is easily recognizable to an audience member. This kind of movement in a dance reminds us we are all human and all move, propelling ourselves through time and space. Simple movement choices can be very strong and provide focus to a dance.

Exercise 4.6
Experimenting with Traveling

▶ Explore walking forward, sideways, and backwards while randomly changing direction. Don't think too hard about the direction you're *traveling* in; allow yourself to be spontaneous. Keep it simple. Just walk and be aware of the different areas of the studio. Focus on rhythm and pace, and frequently change the tempo of your walking.

▶ Add moments of stillness to your walking, time where you just stand still and observe what is around you.

▶ Next, start running. Add a jump here and there as you are running, any kind of jump. Make one up. Add moments of stillness to the running.

▶ Write in your journal about any impressions you had while doing this improvisation.

Gesture and Abstraction

Another part of everyday life often incorporated into dance vocabulary is the concept of *gesture*. An everyday gesture like brushing your hair out of your face or placing your hand on your heart can convey a moment of tenderness or frustration. There are whole dances made of gesture. Choreographers Bill T. Jones and Trisha Brown both produced works based on gesture, as have many other choreographers. Think of the different emotions attached to different gestures and the energy behind a gesture. There's a frantic wave and a casual wave and a happy wave. A foot stomp can be playful or forceful. Gesture can portray a personality or a character – from a self-conscious touch of the hair to a vain primp.

Exercise 4.7
Exploring Gestures

▶ Stand in front of the mirror. Explore as many gestures as you can. Use your whole body to gesture with, not just your hands. Include postures and body stances. Do this for four or five minutes, looking for new ways to perform the same gestures.

You can also abstract a gesture, turning it into a whole other movement. By abstracting a smaller movement into something larger or just a little skewed from its original intent, you add another level to the vocabulary. Think of abstract paintings like those of Picasso, Van Gogh, and Monet. When you abstract a gesture you are still connecting to the essential qualities of the movement. You're not moving so far away from it as to lose its initial intent. You are just expanding or contracting the gesture a bit to move away from its narrative quality and into a more expressive movement.

Exercise 4.8
Experimenting with Gestures

▶ Choose a gesture from your exploration in the mirror. Investigate the potential of that gesture for abstraction by:

- o Making it bigger
- o Making it smaller
- o Performing it with a different body part
- o Performing it while traveling in space
- o Performing it while upside down
- o Making it bigger while you also make it travel
- o Making it as tiny as possible while you are upside down
- o Performing it as you crawl along the floor
- o Combining any of these suggestions and/or making up your own

▶ Do the same investigation with two other gestures.

▶ Make a little ditty using three other gestures and the above abstraction techniques. Choose three or four movements from each exploration and combine them into a short phrase.

Levels in Space

It is important to notice that a dance space is made up of different *levels in space*. When you jump, you penetrate space above the normal, everyday level; the eye raises with the movement and the energy peaks. There is a moment of suspension, an intake of breath, and the realization that the dancer is attempting to defy gravity and fly.

There is also the floor space, where humans first begin locomotion. Gravity is inherent, pressing down and weighing us to the ground. It doesn't mean there isn't momentum and flow on the lower level of the dance space; think of break dancing and hip hop. It just means we are closer to the earth, the floor, and the roots of our beings. We crawl and fall and lie flat, implying a closer relationship to gravity.

Exercise 4.9
Using Levels of Space

☑ **LEARN MORE**

Scan the code or visit
http://bit.ly/AoL4newt

▶ Explore the concept of moving through levels of space using spiraling movement. Contact Improvisation is based on the idea of the *spiral*. The video *Fall After Newton* is a great example of the use of the spiral and levels in space. Find as many ways as possible to move up and down from the floor activating the spiral in your spine. Twisting, twirling, and undulating up and down from the floor to standing.

▶ Add jumps to this spiral dance, going from the floor to jumping and back to the floor.

▶ Continue the dance by using the spiral as you travel through space, moving up and down and jumping. Spiral on the floor, dancing with the floor. Allow yourself to feel how gravity is a part of everything you do and attempt to defy it all at the same time. Enjoy being out of control. Don't choreograph. Instead, center on the concept of moving through space and time, articulating the spiral in your spine and your whole body as you move through all of the levels.

▶ Using your symmetry/asymmetry ditty exercise from this chapter, explore how the phrase can change levels going from either the floor to standing and

jumping, or from jumping to the floor. Don't get attached to keeping the precise movement from the symmetry/asymmetry phrase. Modify the movement to complete your objective. Many new *aha moments* happen when you're fudging and trying to make something work. It could lead you down a whole new path of movement. Listen to your intuitive voice.

Of course, we have the luscious middle space where most dancing takes place. This is where we scoot and sashay, twirl and prance, gesture and hold each other. All of the dance space is important, and each level implies a different emotion and use of the artistic eye in relationship to the audience. Look at the way choreographer Twyla Tharp uses the space or the way choreographer Elizabeth Streb employs the vertical and horizontal space. *Aerial Dancing* is a great example of breathing up and into the vertical space and making gravity-defying movement.

Exercise 4.10
Combining the Shape Elements

▶ In this chapter, you have choreographed three studies: one creating shape with different body parts, one abstracting gesture, and one creating symmetrical and asymmetrical shapes that change levels in space. Combine these three studies into a whole and at some point include some form of pedestrian movement.

▶ The purpose of this final study is to guide you into forming separate pieces into a whole. We're not looking at theme or content yet, but we are practicing process and construction. See what pieces seem to flow together. Arrange the pieces in different orders. Play with the timing of the pieces so, as a whole, there are different dynamics within the study. There is no right or wrong way to construct this. Follow your intuition. Listen to the movement and feel your way through it.

▶ Stay focused on what flows and where something feels stuck. When it feels stuck, let it go, move on, and change your approach. Explore the possibilities, but don't get caught up in making it perfect. It's just a little ditty to play with and learn from. Enjoy it. Nothing is ever perfect. It's a practice in making choices and then examining and learning from them.

Conclusion

To improvise is to take a risk in dance and to dare to break away from the moves you know. It is a way to understand your unique movement vocabulary. You have to focus your energy and become attentive to your movements. Explore the way your limbs move, and experiment with shape, both symmetrical and asymmetrical. Recognize everyday gestures and abstract them into new movements. Try shifting your movement into different levels of space, from the middle space to the floor or in the air. Mix up your vocabulary and change it into something new.

ACC Student Case Study

Lindsay Robinson

To start off the process for what unknowingly would become my final choreographic work at the end of the semester, Darla had us bring to class five gestures of our choice. We brought in gestures and other everyday movements for things like driving a car, reading a book, snapping, looking both ways before crossing the street, and throwing a baseball. Next, we were asked to combine the gestures/movements together in various orders to create new combinations. Following this exercise, I was then paired up with two other dancers to whom I was supposed to teach my gestures and then I would learn theirs. My gestural vocabulary went from five gestures to fifteen! Although the movement did not necessarily look the same on my body as it did on its creator's, I realized, in a matter of minutes, I had what seemed like an endless amount of movement combinations to create a short "study" or dance. This is when the term "movement invention" became a familiar and embodied term.

Darla then asked the class to think of a place, any place, and to describe it in our journals. What does it smell like? Can you taste the air? What does it taste like? What did I see in this place? What textures and colors represented the place? We were asked to cover all the senses to describe our imaginary place. I planted myself in front of a big limestone rock outcrop. After meditating over this place for about ten minutes, Darla asked us to remain there and to then put the gestural work we had developed in this place, to perform our gestural phrases as if we were there.

While imagining I was in the woods next to this large rock outcrop, I realized how much my mini phrase had changed and refined just by making this slight adjustment of place in my brain. All of the present elements – the studio, the lights, the mirrors, bottles of water, etc. – around were no longer present. I was immediately transported to the world I had just envisioned, surrounded by nature and feeling small next to a massive rock. It had the greatest impact on me of all the studies we did because it allowed me to take movement that was already engrained in my muscle memory and add a completely new feel to it. It allowed me to create a place (real or made-up) and develop a character.

This study opened up the vision for what would be my final choreography to present at the end of the semester. When a moment of doubt or a sense of being overwhelmed took over, I was able to approach my block by just simply revisiting my place. This is a study I will recycle and keep ready for use throughout my choreographic development.

Outside Sources

Jazz musicians

- John Coltrane
- Miles Davis
- Bill Frisell
- Terrance Blanchard

Outdoors

- Birds flying in flocks and landing
- Wind blowing leaves and trees
- Clouds forming and changing
- People at a bus stop or a busy street corner

Team sports

- Soccer
- Basketball
- Hockey

Choreographers

- Martha Graham, marthagraham.org
- Merce Cunningham, merce.org
- Katherine Dunham, kdcah.org
- Elizabeth Streb, streb.org

Performances

- Bill T. Jones, *Continuous Replay*
- Trisha Brown, *Accumulation*
- Contact Improvisation video, *Fall After Newton*
- Twyla Tharp, *Push Comes to Shove*

Abstract Painters and Artists

- Picasso
- Monet
- Van Gogh
- Kara Walker
- Damien Hirst

Articles

- Banes, S. "Democracy's Body: Judson Dance Theatre and Its Legacy." *Performing Arts Journal*, 5 (1981): 98-107
- De Spain, K. S. "Dance improvisation: Creating chaos." *Contact Quarterly*, 18 (1993): 21-27
- Martin, N. "Ensemble thinking: Compositional strategies for group improvisation." *Contact Quarterly*, 32 (2007)
- Rainer, Y. (2005). "Some thoughts on improvisation (excerpt) from Work 1961-1973." *Contact Quarterly*, 30 (2005): 32
- Sgorbati, S. "The emergent improvisation project: Embodying complexity." *Contact Quarterly,* Winter/ Spring (2007): 40-46
- Sheets-Johnstone, M. "Thinking in movement." *The Journal of Aesthetics and Art Criticism*, 39 (1981): 399-407
- Topff, N. "Game structures, a performance." *Contact Quarterly*, 5 (1980): 30-31

Books

- Albright, Ann C., and David Gere, eds. *Taken By Surprise: A Dance Improvisation Reader*. Connecticut: Wesleyan, 2003

- Foster, S. L. *Dances That Describe Themselves: The Improvised Choreography of Richard Bull*. Connecticut: Wesleyan, 2002

- Nagrin, D. *Dance and the Specific Image: Improvisation*. Pittsburgh: University of Pittsburgh Press, 1994.

- Tufnell, M., and Crickmay, C. *Body, Space, Image: Notes Toward Improvisation and Performance*. New Jersey: Princeton Book Company Publishers, 1999.

Chapter Terms

Abstract: To consider or perform a movement in a new or original way, apart from what is expected or obvious.

Aerial dancing: A form of dance involving an apparatus attached to the ceiling that adds a vertical dimension to a dance.

Aha moment: The little zing you get inside yourself when you create or discover movements, ideas, or questions that are authentic to your dance and process.

Asymmetry: A non-symmetrical form or body position providing more interest for the eye.

Capoeira: A Brazilian dance of African origin incorporating martial arts movements such as kicks and chops.

Contact Improvisation: An improvised dance based on physical communication between two moving bodies that are in constant contact.

Ditty: A short improvised dance sequence.

Focus: To be attentive to what you are doing and to keep your attention on the task at hand.

Gesture: The use of everyday movements as a means of expression.

Improvisation: The spontaneous choices of expression made consciously or unconsciously.

Levels in space: The physical location of a dance, such as the floor space, the middle space, and the air.

Making choices: Making a conscious decision, whether in life or in dance.

Muscle memory: Physical memory of the movements you execute or create.

Pedestrian movement: Walking, hopping, skipping, standing in place, or running in dances.

Riding the groove: Allowing emotions and personality to come out during the dance and letting the movement lead you.

Spiral: Twisting, twirling, and undulating up and down from the floor to standing.

Stock moves: Movements you find yourself doing repeatedly.

Symmetry: Balanced shape and relative position of the limbs.

Traveling: Movement forward, backwards, or sideways during a dance.

Questions to Consider and Discuss

1. What is the purpose of improvisation in choreography?

2. What are some of the tools that can help you stay focused while improvising?

3. What is muscle memory?

4. How do you know when you are repeating movement you already know?

5. What is a stock movement?

6. What is the difference between symmetrical and asymmetrical shape?

7. What does it mean to abstract a movement?

8. How can using levels in space help to make the space more dynamic?

5 YOUR TOOLBOX

"The creative process is not controlled by a switch you can simply turn on or off; it's with you all the time."

–Alvin Ailey

In this chapter, you will explore:

- Building a toolbox

- Nurturing "aha" moments

- Choosing collaboration

- Asking yourself questions

Constructing Your Toolbox

Your *toolbox* is a metaphor for the *practices* or *self-generated questions* you use as a choreographer. It can be an imaginary space in your mind, a journal entry, or a separate notebook where you create a log of the practices that inspire you and help you to create meaningful choreography. It may even be this book and your notes from the exercises. Each choreographer's toolbox is unique and expressive of the style and dances he or she makes. It is only through making dances that you learn what goes into your toolbox.

The components of your toolbox are as personal as your choreographic process. Using your journal as a way to store insights and information is a good start toward learning what kind of choreographer you are. Maybe you record impressions or images you see as you go through your day, or maybe you keep track of various parts of a study that really seem to speak to you. Taking detailed notes of your work is a good way to begin to analyze what works for you as you develop your own voice.

You may discover certain processes as you are making material. Notes about what kinds of improvisations help you to generate material provide useful information for your toolbox. Jotting down your thoughts also helps you to dig into your work and create new tasks for yourself. Most importantly, listen to your intuition and sense of what works for you and speaks to you about your choreography. Everyone has his or her own way into creating dances, and this can change, even from dance to dance. Your toolbox is just a bag of tricks to help you along the path.

As you go through the exercises and studies in this book, you will get to know your *choreographic style* and preferences and begin to understand what goes into your toolbox. You are the creator of this unique process and will determine through the actual making of dances what works and does not work for you. It is a place where you keep options for yourself. Your toolbox will also evolve through time and creation of your work. Nothing stays the same, including you. Your choreographic style will change with maturity and training. Allowing yourself to evolve and become more aware of these changes helps you to become clearer about what your expressive intention is in your dances.

Exercise 5.1
Investigating Environment through Improvisation

▶ Break into groups of three. Person A leads person B, who is blindfolded, through a variety of experiences, whether outdoors or indoors. Stay in contact to ensure safety.

▶ Person B reports the experience out loud, as person C records the words and impressions. Work together for fifteen minutes before changing roles.

▶ Optionally, do this on your own (without the blindfold). Consider visiting your site a couple of times. Record your experience and impressions in your journal.

▶ Go. Explore. Touch. Listen. Sense. Be near; be distant. Note whatever comes to your attention during your exploration of the organic and inorganic elements of the place you visit:

  o Textures, qualities
  o Contour, shapes
  o Temperatures
  o Sounds
  o Circumstances (up a tree, against a wall, split in two)
  o Sensations
  o Mental images associated with what you are attending to in the environment
  o Movements
  o Making it as tiny as possible while you are upside down

▶ Write or speak without censoring yourself and record everything.

▶ Returning to the studio, explore your movement options with one word or phrase at a time. Keep working; exhaust the possibilities. Surprise yourself with the kinetic content of your findings. If you have a partner, ask them to read your words to you. Your partner may read a word in different voices or in ways reflective of the quality.

▶ Free associate together about the movement without judgment. Dig deep and get specific.

– by Julie Nathanielsz

Aha Moments

The moment you feel in your bones something is right is called an "aha" moment. This is your intuition kicking in, letting you know you are on the right track. Exploring your environment and listening to your body are how you create these moments of clarity. As you are working and exploring, improvising, and creating, you are also listening for what is authentic to you and your dance. These moments come through listening and discovery. You have to put yourself in a working, creative space for these epiphanies to appear. You have to dig and prod and play with movement so you can recognize when there is something true to you.

Exercise 5.2
Searching for the Aha Moment

▶ Take one of your favorite movements from the previous chapter's final study. Manipulate it into something else. Look for the "aha" moment as you explore the movement.

▶ Write down the process you used to discover this new move. Try to remember and list all the ways you thought of to manipulate the movement. This is now part of your toolbox.

It is much easier to string together movements you already know through your training and other dance classes. To get to know your own voice and style you need to work at it. You have to feel and sense what has resonance for you. Whether for a particular movement or a particular process, you must know from your intuitive core that something fits and works for you. No one can tell you what these moments are or what prompts them. You just have to recognize them for yourself.

Collaboration as a Choice

Throughout this book, you are asked to work with other choreography students to construct studies. You are asked to *collaborate*, which involves incorporating more than one voice into the creative process. There is an inherent dialogue involved in collaborating. It is a process where you learn to listen and speak and create all at the same time, and it can be achieved in many different ways. Contact Improvisation, for instance, is a form where dancers are instantaneously collaborating.

Choreographer Bebe Miller improvises in front of her dancers and asks them to "catch" her movement. She then watches her dancers "re-play" her movement back to her and selects versions to work into the choreography. In this way, she collaborates with her dancers.

Exercise 5.3
Collaborating in Creation

▶ Working with a partner, use the warm-up you designed in Exercise 2.5 and create a new one based on the interchange and dialogue as you interact. The intention is to listen and be open to creating something new, not just combining the two warm-ups. It is important to remain open and respectful to each other's ideas. Be sure to answer "yes" first, and exhaust those possibilities before deciding something cannot work. Use each other's material equally, and create and add some new elements to your warm-up collaboration.

Collaboration also happens all the time in the theatre and dance world. When a play is produced, the director works with a set designer, costume designer, and actors to produce a unified vision of the play. Similarly, choreographers collaborate with musicians, set designers, writers, video artists, actors, visual artists, and dancers.

Lauren Tietz, Choreographer

Contact Improvisation (CI) was developed by choreographer Steve Paxton and was first presented as a series of dance performances he directed in 1972 at the John Weber gallery in New York City. An early definition of CI is:

> *"The improvised dance form is based on the communication between two moving bodies that are in physical contact and their combined relationship to the physical laws that govern their motion – gravity, momentum, inertia. The body, in order to open to these sensations, learns to release excess muscular tension and abandon a certain quality of willfulness to experience the natural flow of movement."*
>
> *–Paxton and others, 1979*

☑ **LEARN MORE**

Scan the code or visit
http://bit.ly/AoL5coim

CI can range drastically from meditative and nuanced to wild, athletic, and spacious. Dancers track the movement of their attention, awaken their senses, and mine the body/mind's resiliency and native intelligence. Because CI uses 360 degrees of circular space (sequencing out of the ground and into the partner's support), dancers learn to relate to disorientation and to being upside. One can easily see the artistic parallels between CI and martial arts.

Dancers communicate skin to skin through touch, calibrating and adjusting to the shifting pressure and weight. Through contact, the mass of the body moves through space and into and out of the support of the partner and the floor. A range of movement qualities arises through changing points of contact – counterbalance, sliding, falling, reaching, rising, resting, and flying, for example. An active calibration is required of each dancer to adjust to the compositional and physical forces evolving every second. One learns to become actively awake in the present moment.

Unlike other technical forms of dance where choreographic patterns are mirrored and perfected, CI facilitates a deep listening and tuning into what the organism is capable of instinctively. Because of the nature of the human spine, spiral movement is often accessed to redirect momentum or to generate energy.

CI is also inherently relational as dancers learn to sense what is happening both internally and externally, tracking where one's center of gravity is in relationship to the partner's center of gravity, while noticing preferences and tendencies. The practice is an approach that seeks authenticity rather than a prescribed physical outcome. Dancers also learn to release excess tension, responding to the conditions at hand rather than following prefabricated plans.

The idea of "natural flow" (as quoted above) carries resonances of Taoism, where certain planetary truths (relating to polarities) are revealed and which are also observed in CI. A few principles of importance include the following:

- **Use less effort (often less than we think):** It is easier to redirect momentum than to interrupt it with oppositional force.

- **Harness energy as it rises:** Sometimes it is easier to go down before going up, as momentum can eventually rise up from the force of the downward fall.

- **Let go in order to support**: Grabbing, clinging, trying to stop another's fall – these all lead to possible injury and interrupt the "natural flow." Instead, rather than creating a dead stop, respond with acceptance.

- **Move as a pendulum**: When weight is allowed to swing between poles, gathering the force necessary to change position in space, the flow of movement is easier than expecting a big change from a static position.

As improvisers, we turn our attention to both the science of the body (perception, anatomy, effective balance of effort and ease, the physics that govern our movements) as well as the poetics of movement (the nuanced human choices we make in the moment that reveal narration, emotional relationships, and rhythmic shifts). It is this intimacy of dialogue within the body/mind/spirit and the larger ecosystem that allows for complexity within compositional material in performance.

When you collaborate, you learn to think and listen on your feet. You are given the opportunity to stay open to the creative process in a whole new way. The key to collaboration is to always say "yes" to everything. Go with it, try it, explore it until the end and see where it leads you. Often it transforms into something else and heads in a direction you could not have even imagined. Two voices are riffing off of each other to create a blended third.

Collaboration is not always easy. You have to remember to stay open to the moment and not get too attached to particular ideas. If you feel strongly about a movement or a process, however, acknowledge your feelings and see if you can work it into what you are creating. Just as there is no single way to create your own choreography, there is no right or wrong way to collaborate. It is up to the imaginations of the artists involved to come up with what works for each of them. It does not have to be entirely conscious, either. For instance, Abstract Expressionism, influenced by psychologist

Carl Jung's "collective unconscious" theories, accentuated the artist's ability to subconsciously tap into a shared knowledge of myths and symbols through artistic expression. As long as there is openness and respect for the other's ideas and voice, then collaboration can be a wonderfully unique creative experience.

☑ **LEARN MORE**

Scan the code or visit
http://bit.ly/AoL5nic

Nicole Wesley, Choreographer

Collaborative choreographic structures are like second nature to me. I enjoy the call and response of the process, like two creators playing a choreographic "board game," where every move is initiated and inspired by your game-playing cohort.

One of the most important aspects of collaboration is who you choose as your cohort, or in this case, who you choose to collaborate with. Some questions you might ask yourself before embarking on a collaborative project may include the following: "Does the person you wish to collaborate with understand and appreciate your aesthetic?" "Does he or she encourage and allow you to be yourself throughout the process?" "Do you trust him or her and his or her instincts?" For me, it will not be a successful endeavor unless I have answered "yes" to all of the questions stated above. As most of us know, it is already challenging enough to be vulnerable and formalize movement with your own name on it, so finding the right partner to bare your artistic soul to is as important as the work itself.

Collaboration is about listening. I am constantly aware of what my partner is contributing, how the participants are responding, how the work is forming, and what I could add to this process to ensure it continues to ebb and flow into an eventual moving landscape of succinct ideas that speak to the human spirit. The art of listening connects me to my partner, and because of this resilient and rich connection, I am able to experience a multitude of inspirations as a collaborator and as a choreographer. I can only be directed as a creative contributor to the work if I am sincerely listening to all aspects of the process for that is how true collaboration is respectfully and authentically achieved.

Knowing What Questions to Ask

Questioning yourself is an inherent part of the choreographic process. Asking questions is an important tool in your toolbox. It is essential to discern what questions you want to investigate. Again, it comes down to these basic questions: What moves you to create work? What is it you want to express? How can you be clear about your intention?

There are no right answers to the questions that fuel your choreography. You do not even have to know the answers, but you have to learn to ask yourself the right questions. It helps to be able to articulate to yourself and others what you are trying to explore. Ultimately, the answers to the questions you ask will provide you with material and insight into what you are doing.

Exercise 5.4
Asking the Right Questions

▶ Take time to look at a piece of art, whether it be a painting, sculpture, poem, a dance found online, or just something you are attracted to or repulsed by.

▶ In your journal, start asking questions about the work. Dig into the details and see if you can discover more about the work through the questions you're asking. Use questions starting with the words *why*, *what*, and *how*. Don't judge yourself on whether the questions are simplistic or sophisticated. This exercise is just about beginning to identify what the questions may be.

Investigating a question is like putting it under a microscope and looking at it from all sides and directions. You turn it over on its side; you manipulate the phrasing; you try to peer into it from different angles and perspectives; and you keep poking at it. This is what you do with movement vocabulary and phrases. You turn it upside down. You try it with different body parts. You manipulate the material and find those "aha" moments, and then you add those discoveries to your toolbox. This way, you have a record of what works for you and a place to jump off from for your next study, dance, or collaboration.

Feedback

Learning to give and receive constructive feedback is an important tool for your toolbox, and it is one you will explore in Chapter Six, "Feedback". Ultimately, feedback will teach you more about your process and aesthetics. It will help you to learn how to ask questions of yourself and of other artists.

Conclusion

Your toolbox is comprised of the methods and resources you use as a choreographer. Once you shut down your defeatist voice and learn to listen to yourself, you will have unlimited access to your creative toolbox. You are more open to the collaborative process and learn to think on your feet. You discover what questions to ask during the development of a dance or movement, which allows you to articulate both to yourself and others what you are trying to create. It is also important to give and receive constructive feedback. Feedback generates more questions to help you and others in the choreographic process.

ACC Student Case Study

Tara Baker

A lot of my dance experiences have been one person creates the movements and then the others learn the creation. My partner and I were not too familiar with each other, and we had completely different movement styles. We used movement created from the figure eight and pedestrian movement exercises combined with something we had seen and something we wanted to do, along with the creating our space study. My partner and these exercises ended up being the perfect recipe for a creative, beautiful process. We expanded each

other's vocabulary, allowing us to push each other's boundaries of what we were capable of, while learning from each other. When collaboration takes place many doors open, and not only are you creating a dance with someone, you are also creating a relationship and experiencing all of this together. I made a dance and a lifelong friend at the end of this study.

Outside Sources

Pallant, Cheryl. *Contact Improvisation: An Introduction to a Vitalizing Dance Form.* North Carolina: McFarland & Company, Inc., 2006

Teck, Katherine. *Making Music for Modern Dance: Collaboration in the Formative Years of a New American Art.* New York: Oxford University Press, 2011

Tharp, Twyla. *The Collaborative Habit: Life Lessons for Working Together.* New York: Simon & Schuster Adult Publishing Group, 2009

Olsen, Andrea. *Body Stories: A Guide to Experimental Anatomy.* New York: Station Hill Press, 1991

Chapter Terms

Choreographic style: The flavor of your choreography. The coloring and shadings that make the dance your own.

Collaborate: To include at least one more creative voice in the process of creating a dance.

Practices: Tools, ideas, or questions leading you in the process of choreography.

Self-generated questions: Questions you ask yourself to help you dig deeper into what kind of dance you are trying to make.

Toolbox: A metaphor for how you correlate or keep track of what processes or questions guide you through making a dance.

Questions to Consider and Discuss

1. Why should you have a toolbox?

2. How can you personalize your toolbox?

3. How do you know what goes into the box?

4. How do you determine what is essential to you and your process?

5. Why is knowing the right questions to ask yourself an important part of the process of creating a dance?

6 FEEDBACK

"Dance first. Think later. It's the natural order."

–Samuel Beckett

The Importance of Feedback

For students of choreography, there is no better way to learn how to make a dance than to make a dance. The next important task is learning how to look at your dances and others' dances in a thoughtful and curious manner. This is the way to learn about and investigate your own creative process. Each creator's process is a unique and evolving system used to attain an artistic vision. Useful feedback provides you with the tool of insight, which can then be used to grow as an artist.

Feedback helps you learn to look more deeply into your own work and choreographic process. The

In this chapter, you will explore:

- Having other choreographers look at your work

- Looking at other choreographers' work

- Using Liz Lerman's Critical Response Process

process of feedback involves teachers and other dancers serving as a sounding board for you, reflecting back questions and observations you may have about your choreography. Feedback and criticism are not the same thing. Feedback is the transmission of evaluative or corrective information about an action, event, or process to the original controlling source. *Criticism* is the act of criticizing, usually unfavorably; it is a critical observation or remark.

As a choreographer, you want to be able to look at your work and others' work objectively. It is essential to:

» Engage not only your intuition but also your rational and thoughtful self in the choreographic process.

» Learn how to step back from your work and ask yourself questions.

» Step back from other artists' work and be objective and inquisitive.

In this way, you stay open to the process and stay away from judging yourself and others. Being supportive of someone else's work is helpful for keeping yourself focused on your own dances in a positive manner.

Why Have Others Look at Your Work?

When another choreographer steps back and observes your dance in process, he or she can provide you with insight into what you are trying to express. Having someone else's attention is like shining a spotlight on your work. This can help you clarify your *intention* as you work to ensure the other choreographer clearly understands what you are trying to express.

Exercise 6.1
Seeking Feedback

▶ Based on your experience with Exercise 4.10, make a list of three to five questions about the piece you created. Focus on forming the questions in a way that will encourage a dialogue of feedback regarding your piece, not just a yes or no answer. Using *how* or *what* in your questions along with specific details about the work will help others to provide more informative and objective answers and less personal preference when answering your inquiries.

There must be a sense of openness in the questioning process. When you are asked something from an inquiring place instead of a judgmental place, there is room for discovery and curiosity. Another artist will see something different in your dance than what you are seeing. You are not going to immediately change your work based on this feedback; instead, you are gathering insight, new perspectives. You want to push into the work, to pry and pinch and noodle around with it based on the information you receive. Nothing is so precious it cannot be changed or enhanced to make your dance a stronger whole.

LeAnne Smith, Choreographer

All choreographers need feedback. Most not only need feedback, they seek, welcome, and value the insights it provides. Along with learning the craft of choreography, we also learn the craft of constructive feedback.

My approach to both has changed over the years and may differ in a given set of circumstances. When watching a piece of choreography, I ask to see it twice before I comment. I take notes both times. The first time is reaction. The second is response. Then I phrase my comments in the form of questions. "Why did you choose X?" "Have you considered Y?" "What do you want the audience to see, think, or feel when you ..." "How can you accomplish that goal?" "I'm curious about ..." It is my hope these

☑ **LEARN MORE**

Scan the code or visit
http://bit.ly/AoL6lean

questions will help the choreographer to find his or her own solutions rather than me simply "fixing" the work. I don't want to edit the work. Instead I want the choreographer to become his or her own editor, constructor, or creative problem solver.

It is also not enough to vaguely tell a choreographer, "I like the beginning, ending, etc." Rather, we need to provide concrete reasons why we appreciate or question a part of the product or perhaps the process.

Comments addressing specifics are most helpful. For example, "I enjoyed the asymmetry in the middle section. It was an intriguing juxtaposition to the previous phrase." "It surprised me when the dancers did (fill in the blank)." "Your choice caused me to become more involved in the emotion portrayed by the dancers." Perhaps you say, "It confused me when two of dancers left the stage. Why did you make that choice?" These types of comments allow the choreographer to respond to and refine his or her choreography in his or her own voice and vision.

I have been a choreographer for over thirty years, and I am still learning. The gift of feedback is one I treasure giving and receiving. Many thanks to those who have taken their time and talent to give both equally valuable gifts.

The *process of investigation* creates an opportunity for you to dig deeper into yourself and to explore what you are truly trying to make. It helps you to question yourself in a gentle and curious manner rather than in a harsh and intimidating manner. You will find it so much easier to stay open and connected to what you are making when you are giving your work room to breathe and gently massaging it along.

Why Look at Others' Work?

Taking the time to involve yourself in someone else's process gives you the opportunity to see into another choreographer's way of constructing and thinking about dance. There is no right way to choreograph, no right process. Choreography is an individual act. By watching other dancers and understanding a bit more of the mechanics a choreographer is employing, you can learn more about your own crafting techniques and gain insight into your dance-making. Observing someone else's process is also a way to inspire yourself and gather information about different approaches to some of the same challenges you may be facing in your work.

The important thing is to formulate open-ended, nonjudgmental questions to encourage the choreographer to think about the dance. You want to help your fellow artist to investigate and dig into what he or she is dancing about. Even if the dance is purely about structure, you can still provide insight and help the choreographer define his or her vision. In articulating thoughtful and inquisitive questions about another's work, you are also practicing how to formulate questions for yourself and learning how to investigate and dig into your own dances.

This kind of inquiry through asking *neutral questions* is how you learn to be more objective when watching dance. You can be intrigued and moved by something you do not particularly like. You can be mystified and curious about an artist's process and learn something new by staying open to another's path and choices. You are watching dances and asking questions to learn more about the craft of choreography and what it actually takes to do this creative process.

Liz Lerman's Critical Response Process

☑ **LEARN MORE**

Scan the code or visit
http://bit.ly/AoL6liz

Critical Response Process (CRP) is an invaluable tool for giving and receiving feedback. This codified process is useful not only for choreographers but also for any artistic venture or forum in which people are attempting to give and receive productive and supportive feedback. CRP allows you to dig into your work in an environment with participants who are supportive and interested in what you are making. The process allows you to help others help themselves and in turn teaches you how to look at your own work.

CRP engages participants in three roles:

» The artist offers a work in progress for review and feels prepared to question his or her work in a dialogue with other people.

» Responders, committed to the artist's intent to make excellent work, offer reactions to the work in a dialogue with the artist.

» The facilitator initiates each step, keeps the process on track, and works to help the artist and responders use the process to frame useful questions and responses.

CRP takes place after a presentation of artistic work. Work can be short or long, large or small, and at any stage in its development. The facilitator then leads the artist and responders through four steps:

1. *Statements of meaning*: Responders state what was meaningful, evocative, interesting, exciting, or striking in the work they have just witnessed.

2. *Artist as questioner*: The artist asks questions about the work. After each question, the responders answer. Responders may express opinions if they are in direct response to the question asked and do not contain suggestions for changes.

3. *Neutral questions*: The facilitator asks if the artist would welcome opinions. If the artist agrees, responders ask neutral questions about the work and the artist responds. Neutral questions try to avoid bias or opinions as much as possible. For example, if you are discussing the lighting of a scene, the question "Why was it so dark?" is not neutral. The question "What ideas guided your choices about lighting?" is neutral.

4. *Opinion time*: Responders state opinions, subject to permission from the artist. The usual form is this: "I have an opinion about _____. Would you like to hear it?" The artist has the option to decline opinions for any reason.

For in-depth guidance on how to use and facilitate CRP, see the book *Liz Lerman's Critical Response Process: A Method for Getting Useful Feedback on Anything You Make, from Dance to Dessert.*

Exercise 6.2
Using the CRP Method

▶ Form a small group consisting of three or four choreographers. You will show each other the pieces you created from Exercise 4.10. Before you start, be sure to refer back to Liz Lerman's CRP and bring the list of questions you developed in Exercise 6.1.

▶ Have your journal ready to take notes and write down questions for the choreographer. Remember to form your questions in a neutral way so as to be able to elicit information from the artist and to help them understand better what they are doing and making. Refrain from giving your opinion. Also, be sure to jot down meaningful moments, something interesting, evocative, or exciting.

▶ One at a time, present your piece to the group. After each person's showing, take time to gather your thoughts and questions and to write them down. Use CRP with each choreographer starting with 1) Statements of Meaning and going through to 4) Opinion Time. Using CRP as you work your way through the studies in the book is a valuable way to practice the form and to be ready to choreograph and receive feedback for your final project.

Darla Johnson, Choreographer

I discovered CRP while attending the Alternate Regional Organization of Theaters South (ROOTS) annual meeting. Alternate ROOTS, an organization based in southeastern United States, supports artists who have a commitment to making work in, with, by, for, and about their communities and those whose cultural work strives for social justice.

Performances of all types were presented at the meeting, and after each performance, there was a feedback session in which CRP was being used. It was the first time I came across a process that actually empowered the creator of an artistic work. I began with the process in my own work and in teaching choreography classes. I noticed immediately that it helped create a more cohesive experience and a stronger sense of community. It also helped the choreographers to comfortably begin to look more deeply at their own work.

I have had the pleasure of working directly with Liz Lerman, the creator of CRP, as an artist presenting work where Lerman herself was the facilitator. I have used this process with my own professional company when evaluating programs, performances, dancers, and employees. It has become an inherent part of my own choreographic process. I am continually asking myself questions that will support me in delving into the unknown with my work.

Conclusion

Feedback is an essential part of the choreographic process. When using CRP, consider your statements of meaning and questions for each other as a way to encourage and inspire each other's work. Prepare your own questions about your work, being inquisitive and open to learning something new about your dance. Remember, opinions aren't meant to be negative but encouraging and insightful for the choreographer, helping him or her to dig deeper into his or her own expression and process.

ACC Student Case Study

Gillian Fey

Our class is a community. We have created an open, honest, and natural environment, though it did not begin this way. It became communal through our work and effort to create meaningful dances. We began with exercises designed to get our creativity flowing and ended up down a path that brought us all together. When we performed our dances, it wasn't like we were alone on stage; everyone was there with us because we had put forth the effort to really be involved in each other's choreographic process.

I have seen all of the dances from the beginning "nuggets" to the performance and I know the elements. I have been there to watch the steps and see them grow and form into amazing works of art. We all opened our minds and hearts to help one another. I have learned more about what I am capable of and how I can push myself to be outside the box. I now know how to think like others and to realize sometimes we have to step back and see how our community reacts. It is really important to consciously commit yourself to being a part of something bigger than yourself. It makes for a better mindset and a more conducive environment to take risks.

In the time I spent in this class, I have learned more about my capabilities as a dancer and choreographer, as well as a human being, than anywhere else. This process has changed me in a way I can only describe as amazing. I am truly blessed to have been a part of this class and the community we created together.

Outside Sources

Lerman, Liz and John Borstel. *Liz Lerman's Critical Response Process: A Method of Getting Useful Feedback on Anything You Make, from Dance to Dessert.* Maryland: Liz Lerman Dance Exchange, 2003

Lavender, Larry. *Dancers Talking Dance: Critical Evaluation in the Choreography Class.* Champaign, IL: Human Kinetics, 1996

Liz Lerman Dance Exchange, danceexchange.org

Alternate ROOTS: Arts, Community, Activism. alternateroots.org

Chapter Terms

Critical Response Process (CRP): A tool created by Liz Lerman to receive and provide useful feedback for artists of all kinds.

Criticism: A critical and sometimes unfavorable remark or comment.

Facilitator: Initiates each step in CRP and helps the artists and responders to frame useful questions and responses.

Feedback: Useful information and observations about your choreography given by other artists.

Intention: What you intend to produce or create; the purpose of your dance.

Neutral questions: Questions presented without opinions or bias.

Opinion time: Responders state an opinion about the work with the permission of the artist.

Process of investigation: Paying attention to how you are questioning yourself and others in regard to your process.

Responders: Those committed to the artist's intent to make excellent work.

Statements of meaning: Statements about what is meaningful, evocative, interesting, exciting, or striking in a work you have just witnessed.

Questions to Consider and Discuss

1. What is the difference between criticism and feedback?

2. Why do you need feedback about your choreography?

3. How does providing feedback for others help you with your own creative process?

4. What elements of CRP do you consider the most valuable for your own process?

5. How can asking questions of another artist provide insight and information for his or her work?

6. How can being asked questions provide insight into and information about your own work?

7. When is it appropriate to give an opinion to another artist as part of the CRP?

7 THE SHAPES WE MAKE

"To dance is to be out of yourself. Larger, more beautiful, more powerful."

—Agnes De Mille

Shaping the Choreographer, Shaping the Dance

In this chapter, you will explore:

- Creating shape

- Relating shape with levels in space

- Traveling with shape

- Morphing shape

Dances are made up of shapes and movements braided and strung together. The foundation of any dance is in the movement vocabulary. When you make a dance from the contemporary perspective, you are creating dances from your own *location*. Your location comprises your unique experiences as a human being. You are accessing the physical language you are familiar with or were trained in. You also are tapping into your cultural heritage as well as any other form of physical activity you have spent time doing. From playing sports to rock climbing to skating, all of the different actions and movements you have engaged in live on in your body and muscle memory. All of this is a rich source of choreographic material.

Your body is your tool. Through this tool, your creative choices flow. Every shape and size of dancer is valid and capable of constructing a dance. All of the varied modes of training are valuable to choreographers. There is no right *aesthetic* in the contemporary dance world. The shape of yourself and the shape of your dance are reflections of the cultural worlds you live in today. The rail-thin dancer of the ballet world is an aesthetic in parts of *Western dance* but is not the norm for most dancers around the world. Take, for example, the beautiful and healthy Urban Bush Women, with whom many of us can relate physically. Choreographers create dances from unique and individualized training and perspectives. Influences from every form of popular and cultural dances are seen in today's dance-making. This is what makes it contemporary and what gives you, the choreographer, room to grow and explore.

Peggy and Murray Schwartz, Choreographer and Professor

Someone I find inspiring is Pearl Primus (1919-1994). She was born in Port of Spain, Trinidad, and moved to New York City as a young child. She blazed onto the dance scene in 1943 with stunning works, incorporating social and racial protest into her dance aesthetic. Her work influenced American culture, dance, and education. An early member of the New Dance Group (whose motto was "Dance is a weapon") and a pioneer in dance anthropology, she became an influential international dancer. She traveled extensively throughout the United States, Europe, Israel, the Caribbean, and Africa. She also played an important role in presenting authentic African dance to American audiences.

☑ **LEARN MORE**

Scan the code or visit
http://bit.ly/AoL7prim

Choreographer Rennie Harris and his company Puredance have been creating contemporary hip-hop works since 1992. The collaborative team of choreographers from Headlong Dance Company uses CI and their combined training in gymnastics, theatre, and other dance forms to create works with a vocabulary specific to the theme and content of each of their dances. The *Bollywood* dance company blue13 is a contemporary company whose style is based on traditional Indian *kathak* dance.

The world of dance and the world around you shape the dances you make and your own vocabulary. Exploring and using all of your personal physical information is a fundamental part of contemporary choreography. Draw from your body, other people, props, and everyday objects to influence the dances you make.

Revisiting Shape and Levels in Space

In Chapter Four, "Improvisation and the Unique Voice," you explored how to create shape with different body parts. Remember, the shapes you choose to make help you to define your own unique vocabulary.

Exercise 7.1
A Review of Body Parts

▶ Choose a combination of three body parts. You might choose your right elbow, your spine, and your left leg. Improvise with these three parts, exploring the shapes the three make together. Do not think too much about it; just see what kind of shape you can make while you are having fun.

▶ Spend three to five minutes with this exploration. Remember the shapes or movement of shapes that intrigue and surprise you. Write them down in your journal.

▶ Choose three more body parts. This time it could be your left arm, right shoulder, and hips. Have fun exploring the way these three parts connect and disconnect.

▶ Choose three more body parts and do the exploration again.

▶ Choose two sets of shapes from the three explorations and sequence them together into a whole. Explore the timing and rhythm of each set in order to create internal dynamics inside the whole.

▶ Share your work with others and use the first step of CRP, "statements of meaning."

The level of space through which you move your shapes is another aspect of shape in space. You see many leaps where the legs and arms are held in a shape as the dancer jumps, or you see dancers on the floor holding and sustaining poses. Where your shapes are within a space says something in the dance about that shape. The exaltation of a leap with arms raised and reaching is a different energy than a low jump done with the head down and arms flopping.

Exercise 7.2
Moving Shape Through Levels in Space

▶ Create an asymmetrical shape

▶ Change levels in space, keeping your shape intact. Explore the different levels and *facings* of the shape.

▶ Create another asymmetrical shape and do the same thing.

▶ Create a symmetrical shape on the floor.

▶ Make the shape rise in space to an upright position.

▶ Create another symmetrical shape and then release it to the floor.

▶ Combine these shapes and level changes into one phrase.

Traveling with Shapes

You can *travel through space* with your shapes. Holding a shape as you move through space creates tension and energy in a dance. Slinking around in circles with your arms folded across your chest says something completely different than skipping around the space. Moving through space with your legs bent at right angles is not the same as sashaying with loose limbs. The shapes you make and the energy you bring to those shapes as you travel can portray a multitude of ideas and energies.

Exercise 7.3
Traveling with Shape

▶ Form a shape with your spine and arms.

▶ Run with it.

▶ Run and jump with it.

▶ Twist and fall to the floor with it.

▶ Crawl along the floor with it.

▶ While still on the floor, make a shape with your legs.

▶ Travel along the floor with this leg shape.

▶ Keep the leg shape as you get up and travel through space with it. Hop, skip, jump, slink, quiver, and stumble with the shape intact.

Morphing and Changing Shape

☑ **LEARN MORE**

Scan the code or visit
http://bit.ly/AoL7merc

In all dance forms, dancers morph and change shape in continuous and intriguing patterns as they move through space. The shapes you make and how they transform comprise the vocabulary and language you use to express yourself. Modern choreographers such as Erick Hawkins, Martha Graham, José Limón, and Merce Cunningham all have unique shapes in their vocabulary. Other dance forms such as kathak, *tango*, and *belly dance* all use specific shapes to express their style.

Exercise 7.4

Morphing Shape

▶ Make a shape with the left side of your body.

▶ Morph it over to the right side.

▶ Go back and forth from side to side with the shape.

▶ Make another shape, this time starting with the upper half of your body.

▶ Now translate the shape into the lower half of your body.

▶ Morph it back and forth and up and down.

Transitions

Transitions are the breaths between the shapes and the movements. They are the small moments connecting shapes or phrases together. Alternatively, they may be escalations of energy propelling you into the next moment. Transitions are a mysterious and individual component of choreography. There are no right or wrong ways to transition.

Transitioning is something you learn to do as you choreograph. You begin to create pathways for yourself and tools to guide you into the next shape, movement, or phrase.

A clunky transition between movements or phrases stops the flow of the dance. It can redirect or change the energy or idea. A total shift from the emotion or intention of what you are doing is a strong way of saying, "Now stop looking at that and look at this!" You can think of a transition as the ending sentence of a paragraph, leading you into the next set of thoughts and ideas. The sentences are then all connected, but the process is moving on toward an extension of the information or idea.

Retrograde

Retrograde is when something is moving or performed in reverse. It is taking a movement or set of shapes and rewinding them. Retrograding is a fun and challenging way to explore shapes, movements, and phrases you have already created. It is a way of looking at the material as if through a kaleidoscope, seeing it from different angles and perspectives. Perhaps when you retrograde something, you may even see another color or emotion emanating from the choreography.

The energy and intention of a movement changes as you attempt to rewind it. Think about the difference between running forward and running backward. Try skipping backward. The muscle patterns change, and the dynamics of the movement are different.

Exercise 7.5
Using Transitions and Retrograde

▶ Make five separate shapes. Challenge yourself by creating unfamiliar shapes.

▶ Put the shapes together into one phrase by smoothly transitioning from one shape to the next.

▶ Make sure you are satisfied with how you are moving from one shape to the next. You do not have to place them in the same order you created them. You can even draw numbers randomly to determine the order of the shapes in the phrase. You can always change something.

▶ Now, retrograde or rewind your shape phrase.

▶ Put the two versions of the phrase together, making it into one phrase.

▶ Share the movement with others and use CRP's "statements of meaning" to provide feedback.

Exercise 7.6
Bringing It Together

▶ Review each of the exercises in this chapter, and sequence your notes together into one piece.

▶ You can put them together in any order.

▶ Pay attention to the transitions between each exercise. Make clear choices about how you put together differing concepts and ideas.

▶ Break into groups and share this work with other choreographers, using the CRP method.

Conclusion

There are many aspects to shape in choreography. When you begin to observe your own choices and start recognizing where those choices are coming from, you can start crafting your own unique vocabulary. The quest is to keep exploring and to not be satisfied with something because it feels good or familiar. This does not mean you do not include some of those moves and moments in your work. Instead, you are taking your job seriously as a choreographer to express something from your own unique location.

Remember, you cannot make a mistake. In fact, there is a lot of information in what you may perceive as a mistake. Take the time to listen to what you are making. Observe and ask yourself questions about your intention. Learn to challenge yourself and recognize when you are making the same choices over and over. Choreography is a process, an ongoing and ever-changing series of shapes, movements, energy, questions, and events all making a dance.

Ariel Banos and Lindsay Robinson

This semester I was given the opportunity to create a dance based on an exercise we did earlier dealing with shape. For me, shape means an arrangement or placement of bones, so that's what I thought about. I started to break down each joint to see what body parts can move where. I found some interesting shapes I had never done before. I wasn't sparked with an incredible choreographic idea. I made a phrase I actually was not bummed about, and I decided to keep it and work on it – adding to it, reversing movements, and thinking about timing.

Time was probably the most fascinating factor for me. I feel like it influenced this dance from the get-go. I wanted to construct character roles based on syncopation, which is where I chose to begin the dance. At the start of this process, I honestly had no clue as to what I wanted this to mean. Chelsey started the phrase, and when she finished a portion of the phrase, Yvonne would pick up where she left off while Chelsey moved in slow motion. When Yvonne finished her part of the phrase in regular time, A.G. started the last part of the phrase while Yvonne moved slowly. After A.G. was finished, all the slow motion picked up speed and traveled backward. That is as far as I got for the in-class showings, but I now had movement phrases I could explore and expand upon in the future.

–Ariel

One of the first few exercises we did was an individual study dealing with shapes, from which my final choreographic project spawned. I began playing and creating shapes with my body, and immediately I became interested in looking at positive and negative space. In particular, I focused on moving my body parts in, out, and through the positive and negative space within the shapes I was creating with my body. As we received more direction to advance and string the movements together, I recognized triangles as the common shape I gravitated toward. I explored this shape by finding different body parts that created triangles, creating triangular floor patterns, and researching the number three.

For the next step, I had to add a theme or a motif to the chunks of movement. This was the difficult part for me because I was dealing with inanimate objects; I was dealing with shapes. How do I create emotion with shapes? I drew on the powerful and troubled relationship I was having with my mother. Here is the theme I wrote in my journal:

- build, build, strong, calm
- <strong> down reach out, push away
- build strength, try, put your foot down, try
- what is this movement?
- separate yourself, strong, baby steps
- wash it, wash it
- ahhh

This movement comes from a place of building blocks, the various times in our lives we begin to begin again. There is a sense of struggling with vulnerability and confusion and opposing those emotions; there are ideas surrounding strength and confidence." I realized, shortly after writing this, I could expand beyond the shapes my body made and that everything around me had shape. I also acquired more movement from my nightly dreams and watched various dance videos (in particular Alwin Nikolais for inspiration.

–Lindsay

Outside Sources

Rennie Harris Pure Movement, www.rhpm.org

Headlong Dance Company, www.headlong.com

blue13 dance company, www.blue13dance.org

Alwin Nikolais, www.nikolaislouis.org

Chapter Terms

Aesthetic: Pleasing in a personal way; responsive to or appreciative of what is pleasurable.

Belly dance: A Western term for traditional Middle Eastern dance forms.

Bollywood: A style of dance combining classical Indian dance with contemporary movement and ideas originated in Indian filmmaking.

Facings: The directions the dancers are facing.

Kathak: Classical dance form from Northern India.

Location: The personal and cultural place from which you create.

Retrograde: When movement is performed in a backward direction; a rewinding of choreographic movements.

Tango: A dance form originating in Buenos Aires.

Transition: The minute breaths between shapes and movements in choreography.

Traveling in space: Movement traveling through space.

Western dance: Dance forms and styles from the European tradition.

Questions to Consider and Discuss

1. What defines your own aesthetics?

2. What shapes are new for you, and which ones originate in your training?

3. What does it mean to create from your own location?

4. How can you change or influence your own location?

5. How does traveling with a shape change it, or does it?

6. What is the significance of transitions?

7. How can the use of retrograde enhance or change the movement?

8 THEME

"If I could tell you what it meant, there would be no point in dancing it."

—Isadora Duncan

What Moves You

In this chapter, you will explore:

- Finding your authentic voice

- Investigating a concept or theme

- Recognizing what you want to express

- Relating the quality of movement to theme

A *theme* is a springboard out of yourself and into your dance. It is something to wrap your vocabulary around as you get into the studio and start choreographing. It is an idea to investigate and ask questions about as you make movement. It can be like glue that binds you to the page and focuses your energy toward a specific expression. Theme can be defined as a subject or topic of discourse or of artistic representation. *Concept* is like theme but more abstract and can be defined as:

1. Something conceived in the mind

2. An abstract or generic idea generalized from particular instances

Contemporary choreography as an artistic expression is grounded in the voice of its creators. Connecting to something you are yearning to express is a valid and valuable way to begin the choreographic process.

The early pioneers of modern dance – Isadora Duncan, Loie Fuller, Ruth St. Denis, and Ted Shawn – all choreographed with a thematic or conceptual intent. Some of their works were more theatrical, while others were abstractly expressive of a theme, concept, or emotion. The generation of choreographers after them set the foundation for the expressive choreography still prevalent today. You can find works by Martha Graham, Doris Humphrey, Katherine Dunham, and numerous other choreographers in libraries and on the Internet. You can also look for more contemporary works by Bill T. Jones, Donald Byrd, Margaret Jenkins, Joe Goode, O Vertigo, Sankai Juku, Pina Bausch, Tere O'Connor, the Rosas dance company, and a plethora of American and international artists. You can also attend live dance performances.

Dance-making is happening all over the planet, and looking at other artists' work is an invaluable education you can engage in on your own time. There is always something to be inspired by when you are watching someone else's dance, even if it is only to help you define what you want or do not want your dances to look like. Imitating another choreographer's work is a form of flattery and also a way of figuring out how to develop a dance.

The process of asking yourself what motivates you to move is what will help you decide what to make dances about. There are no right or wrong ideas or themes. If you are authentically engaged with something and can creatively express it through dance, then it can become a dance work. Discovering your theme is about looking inside yourself and noticing what you feel connected to, what about life is captivating to you. It is also about looking outside yourself at the world around you and asking the same questions: What is alluring and mysterious? What is exciting and inviting? What do you want to spend time investigating in both your inner and outer worlds?

José Luis Bustamante, Choreographer

My work is essentially theme oriented. The structure, movement material, and design come out of the exploration of a particular subject that triggers a central idea. The work evolves from this departure point in directions to intensify, contrast, extend, and clarify the central idea. My work is also deeply personal and expresses a vision that comes from a process of internal search. The subjects of my dances must find a place inside of me and must establish a partnership with my heart.

When I engage in the process of creating a dance, I feel as if my consciousness sharpens and becomes deeply receptive, triggering a process of creating and establishing connections around the subject and generating impressions, images, and pathways of knowing. As all of these elements accumulate, the work begins to find its own way, revealing itself in the process. In this journey, as my consciousness unfolds and uncoils, I feel compelled to embody this inner dance and moving intelligence, which seeks physical organization through a form or a vessel to house its expression. So much of what attracts me to the creation of a dance relates to finding or designing the vessel, understanding its function, and discovering the surprises of its workings. It is ultimately a curiosity of how things are put together, of how we make something from "nothing."

Your Authentic Voice

In Chapter Four ("Improvisation and the Unique Voice"), you learned how to improvise to create vocabulary. Improvisation is an important tool to help you discover your authentic voice. Your *authentic voice* defines your style and gives you a foundation to work from. Your body is your voice, and theme and concept guide you to what you want to say. You should ask yourself, "What am I passionate about? What moves me and *resonates* with me?" Something that resonates with you will give you energy and send vibrations through your being. It will get you excited and inspired and make you want to delve in and explore.

Exercise 8.1

Investigating Theme: Passionate Versus Dispassionate

► Make two lists on a piece of paper. The first list is of five things you feel passionate about. The second list is five things you feel dispassionate about. Give yourself plenty of space on the paper between each idea.

► Tear each item on the list into its own separate piece of paper. Fold each piece, keeping the piles separate.

► Randomly pick one from your "passionate" pile. In your journal, define the elements. Break them down into what details evoke your passion. What senses are engaged? Are there smell, texture, color, and visual images? What emotions do you associate with the item? Are there gestures that embody the thing you are passionate about?

► Now, keeping the idea in mind, improvise on each of the elements listed in your journal. Take your time to listen and feel for what rings true to your concept. Pay attention to what movement has energy and creates a visceral feeling for you.

► Discern whether there is something there for you to work with. If so, string some of the movement ideas together, making them into a few short phrases.

► Now, pick something from your "dispassionate" pile and follow the same instructions.

► Follow this same format, choosing two to three times from each pile.

► Break into groups and share this work with other choreographers, using the CRP method.

Right Movement Versus Familiar Movement

What you want to start thinking about in relationship to theme and concept is the idea of *right movement* versus *familiar movement*. Familiar movement is the vocabulary we already know from various technique classes. Right movement rings true and is created from the source of your inspiration for your dance. Discerning between the two is important work. When you recognize you are repeating the same movement patterns, you can then choose how you guide your exploration into creating the right movement for the theme or concept you have chosen. No movement choice is wrong; there are just some choices more authentic than others. These choices feel new and energized and help you to define your voice.

Exercise 8.2
Trying Another Approach

▶ Find a poem that resonates with you.

▶ Pick three images from the poem.

▶ Improvise on each image, allowing yourself to connect to its visual and emotional contexts. Look for right-feeling movement. Close your eyes and move. Do not use the mirror.

▶ Memorize the movements you like by repeating them over and over until they become familiar.

▶ Pick up three movements from each image, nine in total, and weave them together.

- ▶ Repeat the movements, exploring the rhythm from each piece of vocabulary to create a short dance.

- ▶ Break into groups and share this work with other choreographers, using the CRP method.

Recognizing Your Expression

Sometimes you do not know what it is you are trying to say. There is a nebulous, shadowy place where images and thoughts you cannot quite get to reside. It is a dream or a vision, a taste or a feeling of something you have not quite named. One thing you can do when this happens is to go into the studio and move. Do not think about it; do not judge or hesitate. Allow yourself to explore the feelings as they come to you, moving away from the shadowy place. Afterward, use your journal to sift through and dig around for ideas and themes.

Exercise 8.3

Using Your Journal to Explore a Theme

▶ Start by forming a few questions for yourself. Here are some general ideas to start with:

    o What things seem impossible to make a dance about? Make a list.

    o What are you afraid of expressing or exploring? Make a list.

    o What mundane feelings float in and out of your everyday life? Make a list.

Remember, these are your questions, and you can be fearless and honest in your exploration of them.

▶ Pick something from your musing.

▶ Imagine the elements: What kind of music do you associate with the theme, if any? What colors do you identify with this theme? Do you see light? Could the dance be in a nontraditional performing space? What kind of costumes? How many dancers? Is it a solo? Is it an improvised or set work? Can you make a score for it?

▶ Share your dance with another student or in a small group, allowing for discussion and input.

Quality of Movement and Theme

Quality of movement is like adding shading to a drawing. You can use varying qualities to add depth and nuance to a theme or concept for a dance, which will then help define the choreography for yourself and your dancers. Consider how languid, slow movement suggests something very different from sharp, staccato movement. Smooth and flowing qualities create a different intention than jagged and angular movement.

The quality of movement enhances the effect of the vocabulary and suggests a more complex relationship between the movement and the dancer. This allows the audience more insight into what is going on other than what the movement itself is suggesting. It is the energy behind and underneath the movement. It informs the vocabulary with energy and emotion. Quality of movement colors the choreography, creating different intentions for different parts of the overall dance.

Exercise 8.4
Adding Qualities

▶ Make a list of at least ten different qualities of movement.

▶ Choose three qualities from your list.

▶ Use your notes from the poem exercise earlier in this chapter and perform the dance three separate times, each time adding one of the qualities to it.

▶ Now blend the three qualities into the dance so there are different qualities within the same piece.

▶ Break into groups and share this work with other choreographers, using the CRP method.

Conclusion

Creating a dance from a specific theme or concept in mind is a helpful way to clarify your intention. Dances are made from a variety of directions and inputs and can start from something as simple as wanting to make an eight-count phrase on how you feel after walking out of a dance class. Your job as a contemporary choreographer is to express something inherent in your being or something you feel strongly connected to, which can be anything. Being authentic to your own artistic voice is what is important.

ACC Student Case Study

Chelsey Jones

I first came up with my list of passionate and dispassionate items, separating them into two piles as instructed. I then proceeded to choose one from each pile. Since lunch was almost here, I happened to choose mushrooms and onions from the passionate and tomatoes from the dispassionate. I started off with improvising with the passionate items.

My body motions reflected the pan with the onions and mushrooms being tossed in it. I then began to make the shapes of the items and what they would be doing in the pan with my body. While I was dancing, I began to smell and even feel as if I were eating mushrooms and onions.

When it came time to do the dispassionate item, the tomato, I started off by creating circular movement, mostly strong and hard like the outer layer of the tomato. Then I began to work into more fluid movements to symbolize the inner part of the tomato. While doing the exercise, I was able to find different movements I normally did not do.

As I kept doing the exercise, I found, throughout the process, it was easier to improvise on the dispassionate pile than it was to do the passionate. This was a good exercise. It helped me find new movement and explore different types of movements.

Outside Sources

Websites for the choreographers mentioned in this chapter include O Vertigo (www.overtigo.com), Pina Bausch (www.pina-bausch.de), and Tere O'Connor (tereoconnordance.org)

Historical film footage from the pioneers of modern dance on YouTube, including Helen Tamiris' *How Long Brethren* and Sankai Juku's butoh performances

☑ **LEARN MORE**

Scan the code or visit
http://bit.ly/AoL8juku

Poetry books, including *In Search of Duende* by Federico Garcia Lorca and *Complete Poetry* by Oscar Wilde

Poetry websites, including *The Writer's Almanac* (writersalmanac.publicradio.org)

Dance history books such as *Ballet and Modern Dance* by Susan Au and *Ballet and Modern Dance: A Concise History* by Jack Anderson

Chapter Terms

Authentic voice: The choreographer's true expressive voice. An individual's style and vocabulary that defines his or her authentic expression.

Concept: Underlying idea for a dance; the broader element that permeates and influences the movement vocabulary.

Familiar movement: Familiar movement vocabulary easily repeated from having executed it repetitively or studied it.

Quality of movement: Executing vocabulary with a shaded or enhanced intention; adding a layer of complexity to the movement by adding a quality or emotion.

Resonate: A sense of knowing something; movement that rings true or feels right.

Right movement: Movement vocabulary true to the choreographer's intention for the theme or concept chosen.

Theme: The foundation of a dance, the idea driving a dance; a subject or topic of discourse for expression.

Questions to Consider and Discuss

1. What are theme and concept in regards to choreography?

2. How do you know when something resonates with you?

3. What is the difference between movement that feels right and movement that feels familiar?

4. What is quality of movement?

5. How do intention and theme go together?

9 THE MUSIC OF TIME

"Both the music and dance can stand alone and be performed independently, but both are juxtaposed and related instant by instant, movement by movement, and sound by sound, rhythmically from beginning to end."

–Erick Hawkins

Music and the Dance and Time

In this chapter, you will explore:

- Using music as inspiration

- Using energy and theme as motivators

- Creating a landscape or soundscape with music

Music and dance are intertwined throughout history. Nothing gets your heart pumping and your body aching to move like an incessant beat. People all over the world are inspired to move when the music is just right at gatherings from drum circles to raves. Music and sound are driving forces, motivating dancers to choreograph. Dances of all styles and forms are connected to interpreting music with movement and gesture. The beat and syncopation of a Michael Jackson song can be counted and moved to as easily as a Django

Reinhardt swing song. Even classical music can be danced to by modern choreographers. For instance, choreographer Mark Morris is known for his musicality and relationship with classical music.

There are many ways to use music, time, and sound beyond the traditional approach of dancing to the music or interpreting the music. In contemporary dance, music is often the last element added to the work. Dances are made based on ideas and emotions. These, and not the music, are used as the driving force behind the dance. In the contemporary dance world, music is sometimes not even heard by the dancers until they are performing the dance. Choreographer Merce Cunningham and composer John Cage had a unique relationship during their many years of collaboration. They worked independently of each other – Cunningham choreographing the dance, Cage composing the music, and then the two elements coming together only at the performance.

Making Choices About the Role of Music

Music can be an invaluable source for inspiration. There is so much easily accessible recorded music upon which a dancer can draw. Often a song gets stuck in your head and you just want to dance to it. You relate to something in the lyrics or the words seem to speak directly to you. The inclination is to emulate the song. When you do this, the song often dictates the emotion and the movement. You are physically interpreting the song. That is not to say great dances are not made to music with lyrics. For novice choreographers, however, it is best to shy away from what is so easily and literally emoted. In order to dig deeper into yourself as a dance maker and artist, it is best to focus first on developing your choreographic voice and unique movement style. This is a different kind of focus – not away from music but toward yourself.

Exercise 9.1
Playing With Lyrics

▶ Choose your favorite song with lyrics.

▶ Improvise by physically interpreting the lyrics with your movement.

▶ Start the song over. This time, improvise by interpreting only the emotion you feel from the song.

▶ Without the music, dance what you can remember from both improvisations, using your muscle memory.

▶ Notice what movement feels authentic and resonates with you. Record your observations in your journal.

All through your training, in all types of dance classes, you have been taught to count the music and the steps. The beats and rhythms of dancing have been dictated through the music. Choreographers have different relationships and approaches to time. Some dancers count in the same way musicians do. Other choreographers use music to measure time or create rhythm. Another, more contemporary approach is to listen to an internal rhythm or clock, using neither counting nor music. Consider such dance companies as Stomp or Blue Man Group, both of which use rhythm within their choreography. There is such beauty in the syncopation of time and music's relationship and such satisfaction in the two forms harmonizing.

Michelle Nance, *Choreographer*

When choosing music, decide what role your music will play in your choreography. Music can interact with dance as follows:

- Enhances (has a conversation with) your dance
- Dictates your dance
- Juxtaposes your dance
- Ignores your dance

All of these choices are acceptable as long as you know why you have made the choice. Here are some other basic rules to follow:

☑ **LEARN MORE**

Scan the code or visit
http://bit.ly/AoL9mich

1. Music should not be vernacular (for instance, pop music, easily identified). Exceptions: you are doing a parody of the music and/or what it represents; there is a compelling artistic reason the dance will not work without it.

2. It is preferable for your music not to have lyrics, unless they are minimal/abstract or in a foreign language most of the audience will not recognize. If the words are in a foreign language, make sure you have translated it and know the meaning of the music. Music with lyrics can be considered if you have a very compelling argument as to why the lyrics are imperative to your dance.

3. Music in which the voice is used as an instrument, rather than a vehicle for meaning, is okay (for example, Meredith Monk).

4. Music needs to be challenging, not overly lulling.

5. Be careful with soundtrack music; it can be overly dramatic or "sectional."

6. Music should not overpower your dance in terms of dynamics, instrumentation, or rhythmic structure.

7. Consider silence, live music, or originally composed music as a viable option.

8. Consider a "sound score" or text (spoken or recorded) as a viable option.

Do not be afraid to move on with your choreography without music or to switch the music as many times as needed throughout the process. Do not get attached to the rhythmic structure (for example, all eights) and therefore not be able to accommodate the movement to another structure if you change music later on.

What are other ways to think about the music and dance relationship? Challenge yourself to try something crazy! This is your time to be experimental.

There are other ways to relate to music while dancing and choreographing. You can ride the music like a wave, instilling your own internal rhythm into the movement on top of the music and finding harmony and syncopation in the ebb and flow. You can count your movement separately from the music or not count at all. You can feel the energy of the movement vocabulary and the meaning behind it and then lay the music on top or underneath it. You can play with the music, creating a relationship with contrast and space between and around it. To do this, you might need to *dance without counts*. Then, you can find the *internal music* and rhythm of the movement and feel the shifts and changes in dynamics present in the choreography.

It becomes trickier to stay together with dancers as you let go of counts and connect to the movement without them. Dancing without counts establishes a different kind of relationship onstage between the performers. You must rely on your other senses of sight, sound, and touch to stay connected to each other. You must use your peripheral vision and be conscious of where you and the other dancers are in time and space. In this way, you are creating a community in the performance space. Through time, space, and movement, you are connecting to the dance. You are not dancing to the music; instead, you are dancing *with* the music.

Exercise 9.2
Dancing Without Counts

▶ Find a piece of music without lyrics, something at least three minutes long.

▶ Make a list in your journal of the emotions and qualities of the music.

▶ Make another list of the contrasting qualities of the music.

▶ Improvise to the music, using the list of contrasting qualities for movement inspiration.

▶ From the improvisation, put together a phrase, picking and choosing movement from the improvisation.

▶ Dance the phrase with the music while counting.

▶ Dance the phrase along with the music without counts, just feeling the motion of the music.

▶ Teach the uncounted phrase to two other dancers, expressing your internal rhythm, emotion, and sense of the movement. Record your observations from this exercise in your journal.

Energy and Theme as Motivators
Versus Music as Motivator

There is an internal music, an internal rhythm and energy, in your dancing body. You feel it when you are just humming along in your life, walking down the hallway, stirring a pot, washing your hands, showering, walking the dog, or petting the cat. The music is your engine revved up and moving through life.

When you choreograph without moving to music, you start to really feel your internal engine. You can start to play with dynamics and qualities inside your vocabulary and create your own unique phrases. The way you perceive time is different from how everyone else does, and it has more to do with the time it takes to express something than the time dictated by the music. This is trickier than choreographing by moving to music and takes a different kind of focus and commitment from you. It requires you to dig deep inside and not emulate another artist's work.

In Chapter Eight ("Theme"), you explored different ways to create dance from your own ideas and emotions. A dance can also be performed in silence, allowing the audience to follow the choreographer's intention of creating a rhythm and energy to enhance the theme of the dance. Think tap dancing and flamenco. The whole dance can be choreographed without one bit of music and performed exactly the way the choreographer intended the dance to be heard. As mentioned at the beginning of this chapter, music can also be added later after the dance is choreographed, as in the collaborative work of choreographer Merce Cunningham and composer John Cage.

Exercise 9.3
Listening to Your Internal Music and Theme

▶ Refer back to your notes from Exercise 9.2.

▶ Find three very distinct pieces of music.

▶ Try the study with each piece of music, playing with the way the music interacts with the dance.

▶ Perform each one for the class.

▶ Break into groups and use CRP to share feedback about the differing versions of the phrase.

Another way to think about the music for a dance is to devise the rhythm from concept. With this method, you create an internal music by enhancing the theme or subtext of the dance. Think of storms, waves, and the building sound of a train's engine as it gains momentum. Leaves falling, grass being mowed, the splashes of a city bus as it swooshes by are all energies and rhythms you can use underneath a set of movements.

Music as Landscape

The world is a complex and lively place. At any given moment, five things are happening in your environment at the same time. You are texting, watching television, or writing an article while someone next to you is talking on the phone or eating. This is all part of living in our time. Music is everywhere as background sound in your hectic environment – the click-click of computer keys, the drip of a coffee maker, the steaming tea kettle, and the background hum of a television. *Music as landscape* is just a way of saying the music is present and part of the whole as a tool to enliven and highlight the choreography.

Music can provide a backdrop to dancing, similar to having a set onstage for a play. In a play, the set supports the words, emotions, and actions being performed. Music and choreography can be approached in the same way. The music can play the role of supporting the choreographer's vision, serving as the *audio landscape*.

The choreographer's vision can be the driving force of the dance, while the music, costumes (see Chapter Eleven, "Elements of Theatre"), and dance vocabulary can be the supporting elements. There is a balance being created when music is chosen for its ability to enhance the choreographer's intention. Energy is at play, asking audience members to pay attention not only to what they are hearing and seeing but also to both the piece in its entirety and each of its components. Each factor plays a role in supporting the concept of the dance.

Starting a dance based on a theme and without choosing music first is a way to ensure you, the choreographer, are driving the artistic vision. It is good to use all kinds of different music as inspiration in the initial stages of choreographing and to make a dance or a whole bunch of movement phrases just from the concept or emotion you want to express. You can make a whole dance and then bring the music in and connect the two together; there is no wrong way of doing it. There are endless ways you can include and use music with choreography.

Creating a Soundscape

A *soundscape* is something you, the choreographer, hear as background for your dance. It can be the cry of a gull, a train whistle, rain falling, the monotonous squeak of a swing moving back and forth, or the highway traffic you can only hear at night when all else is quiet; it is all of this and more. It can be a blend of sound and music. It can be a compilation of contrasting music and sound. It can be a voice-over of a story your grandmother told you. It can be random voices heard at the mall or the grocery store. It can be your dancers telling you about their lives.

Exercise 9.4
Using the Computer to Make a Soundscape

▶ Choose three pieces of recorded music or sound.

▶ Identify a short section of each piece that speaks to you.

▶ Put them together into one blend of sound. You can use software like Audacity or Mixcraft, or you may choose to call on a friend to help you.

Contemporary dancers all over the world are making soundscapes for dances. Choreographers collaborate with musicians and colleagues on the sounds they hear for dances. This is not a new concept. Choreographer George Balanchine worked with commissioned composer Igor Stravinsky to create music for his ballets, and choreographer Marius Petipa worked with composer Pyotr Tchaikovsky. You may have a friend who is a musician who could create the music or sound for your dance. Computers are also unbelievable resources for creating your own soundscape or musical score. There are computer programs available to mix and blend music easily.

☑ **LEARN MORE**

Scan the code or visit
http://bit.ly/AoL9allm

Michelle Nance, Choreographer

When looking for music, the first place I look is allmusic (allmusic.com). When you go to the website, you'll see a horizontal bar you can use to search by genre. You can listen only to samples from the CDs, and the samples are very short. If you want to hear the whole piece, search for the song or artist on Amazon.com, for example.

- Click on *Jazz*, and you will find all kinds of wonderful subcategories such as *Early Creative* and *Post-Bop*.

- Click on *World* for all kinds of music from Africa to China and beyond.

- Do not be afraid to give *Classical* a chance. Classical music is not just lulling music used for ballet. There are many subgenres in classical, including avant-garde, which can be dissonant, edgy, and strange! Film music and soundtracks are also under the category of *Classical*. Chamber music is also nice for smaller groups.

- If you click on *More*, you can search by mood or theme. This is fun. If you have an idea for your mood, you can search through adjectives such as *giddy*, *rowdy*, or *hedonistic*. Themes include *Reflection*, *Breakup*, *Background Music*, and *Jealousy*.

If you are interested in MP3 blogs as a source for music, I would recommend the MetaFilter (metafilter.com/34264/MP3-Blog-Roundup) and The Hype Machine (hypem.com), both of which offer roundups for MP3 blogs. For a good example of one of these blogs, check out 3Hive (3hive.com). If you would like to learn more about this blog phenomenon, Wikipedia has a Web page providing a brief overview (en.wikipedia.org/wiki/Mp3_blog).

You can also find contemporary, nonmainstream music at Weird Music (weirdmusic.net). Try the library for music recordings and scores. Do you have a friend or classmate who always seems to listen to unusual and interesting music? Have him or her make a playlist for you. Musicians and music students can also point you in the right direction if you are stuck.

If you want something truly original, put up a note in your institution's music building to find a music student who might want to write or play something for your piece. It could be performed live or recorded. Music students probably also have a lot of music already recorded you could listen to.

Like the music you heard in a movie? Make a note of the composer's name and see what other pieces you can find by him or her. Like the music you heard at a dance concert? Save the program and see what other pieces of music you can find by the same composer.

Exercise 9.5
Bringing it Together

▶ Choose two studies from this chapter or previous chapters.

▶ Partner with one or two choreographers and combine your studies, using intuition to integrate them together in a creative way.

▶ Use the soundscape you created in Exercise 9.4 as the music for this material. If there is more music than movement, repeat movement phrases. If there is more movement than music, either start the piece in silence or end it in silence.

▶ Use CRP to provide and receive feedback on this study. Think of this as a mini dance you have created to prepare yourself for your final project.

ACC Student Case Study

Claire Andersen-Wyman

Every time I change music for a dance, the dance itself changes, and sometimes that is really frustrating. If I really like where the dance is and how it's progressing and I'm asked to explore other music options, it can seem like all of the work I did so far was worthless. It is infuriating at times. Rather than give up, I try to take that energy and use it to fuel the dance.

The first solo I choreographed was a similar situation. I went through at least fifteen pieces of music, trying to find the right music. It was the week before the show, and I still didn't have music. I was mortified I wouldn't find anything in time. I used my annoyed/terrified energy to continue working on the dance, which made the movements more intense.

One of my teachers saw the change and suggested an artist, so I went to a music store to find the artist. Unfortunately, they didn't have anything of hers. I explained my situation to an employee of a record store, and she helped me find a few things. One was perfect. It was a good learning experience for me because it forced me to allow myself to be out of my comfort zone.

Outside Sources

- Explore genres of music you are not familiar with.

- Listen to other people's music, especially people whose age is different from yours.

- Explore the iTunes Store and Spotify.

- Listen to movie soundtracks.

- Listen to the sounds around you, whether you are outside or inside.

- Seek out original music from other students and friends.

- Explore music software like Garage Band from Apple, Mixcraft from Acoustica, and Audacity.

Chapter Terms

Audio landscape: Sound or music supporting the theme or concept of the dance as the choreographer envisions it; a part of the overall theme of the choreography, not the driving force.

Dance without counts: To choreograph phrases without counting the music or the steps while following an internal dynamic or rhythm.

Internal music: The rhythm or energy the choreographer feels while choreographing without music.

Rhythm from concept: Using the energy of a concept for the dance to create the underlying rhythm of the movement.

Soundscape: The music or sound created for a particular dance.

Questions to Consider and Discuss

1. Describe the ways in which you can use music in relationship to choreography.

2. How can music be different from just something you dance to?

3. Why should you avoid literally interpreting music, especially music with lyrics?

4. How does choreographing without music inform the choreographic process?

5. Explain the difference between choreographing to your internal rhythm and counting the music.

6. What are the skills you and other dancers use to stay together as an ensemble when not working with counts?

7. How does an audio landscape or soundscape provide another dimension to the dance?

10 SPACE AND THE ARCHITECTURE OF DANCE

"Dance is the only art of which we our-selves are the stuff of which it is made."
                                        –Ted Shawn

Space as Texture

Space is all around and has a living presence. It is the place where your dance lives. Your movement, concepts, and emotions are expressed in this terrain. As you transverse space, you become an architect of sorts. Space has texture, just as your movement has quality. Your vocabulary and the choices you make about how you choose to travel through space help to shape and create the texture of the whole dance. Envisioning the texture of the space as you move through it adds a subtext to the dance and enlivens the space through which you move.

In this chapter, you will explore:

- Using negative and positive space

- Finding and creating focal points onstage

- Defining the shape of the space

- Creating a spatial/movement score

- Developing your imaginary space

A solo versus an ensemble piece also affects how an audience sees the space and how the dancers feel it. A duet, just by the nature of two dancers moving, creates a symmetrical shape to the space. A trio can create triangles, which has an inherent tension, and a quartet gives a square or boxlike feel to the space. Imagine the dance space filled with fifty dancers – maybe the Radio City Rockettes from New York City. The energy between that many dancers is felt both on and off the stage.

☑ LEARN MORE

Scan the code or visit
http://bit.ly/AoL10pav

Carolyn Pavlik, Choreographer

Following in the footsteps of their predecessors, the modern dance choreographers of the 1960s explored new ways of creating and looking at dance. They began taking their art outside of the confines of conventional theatres and into the urban landscape. Dances were created in alternative spaces such as in alleyways and empty swimming pools, on tall buildings and construction scaffolding. These kinds of works became known as site-specific, or site, dances. Site-specific dances are created and performed at a particular place or site; they are not just dances choreographed in a studio and placed on a site.

The location influences the artistic process from the very beginning. Choreographers and their collaborators investigate and take in the site in many ways, including visually, aurally, kinesthetically, and intellectually and then respond to its distinctive characteristics. The site's architecture or topographical features, history, use, or community may inspire the choreographers and serve as guides to inform their artistic choices, such as movement, theme, and music. These dance works are so inextricably linked with the site that, if performed elsewhere, they would lose their original context and have to be adapted to the new site.

In recent years, there has been a resurgence of interest by some choreographers in creating site-specific dances, and a growing number of site-specific dance companies have been established. They have produced works in increasingly diverse places such as parking structures, county jails, soon-to-be-demolished hotels, grain elevators, and industrial cranes. In an anthology I co-edited with Melanie Kloetzel, *Site Dance: Choreographers and the Lure of Alternative Spaces*, sixteen site dance choreographers and artistic directors reveal their attraction to site dance and discuss their individual processes in making these dances.

Although these choreographers have varying approaches, they all value the ability to connect to their communities through their artwork and, due to the great number of the works occurring in public settings, to increase visibility and accessibility of dance to a broader and more diverse audience. They are also interested in providing an opportunity for audiences to experience and engage with their surroundings in new ways. Whether this means highlighting familiar places in new ways or revealing or reintroducing unexplored, abandoned, or forgotten places, they want to disrupt habits of perception and help create new memories or thoughts about a particular place or even the people who inhabit the place.

Some site choreographers strive to bring out multiple readings of places and offer alternative narratives or histories than are generally told or documented about a specific site. Others aspire to reveal the location's natural beauty or want to bring attention to the problems or issues surrounding a site or its community. In this way, their site-specific dances can serve as platforms for social, political, and environmental activism, and aid in increasing awareness of and proposing new solutions for local and global issues. As novice and professional dance artists continue exploring alternative territories for dance and engaging with their communities, different possibilities and innovative discoveries can emerge.

Negative and Positive Space

As with sculpture and other art forms, there is both *negative space* and *positive space* in dance. Negative space surrounds the shape the body is making as it sits or moves in space. It is the unoccupied, empty space. Yet it also provides a shape in itself, as it is confined within the boundaries of the performing space and then functions as shape in the total design. There is energy in the space left unfilled, not just in the space occupied by dancers.

Positive space describes the actual form the dancer is making. The angles and curves, the extensions and stillness of the dancer's body define the positive space. The density in this space anchors the viewer to the dance. When you look at or are choreographing a dance, there is something being said in the space around the dancers as well as in the shapes they are making.

Exercise 10.1
Exploring Shapes in Space

▶ All the dancers should form a large circle in the space. Limit the amount of dancers in the circle to five so there is enough stillness, awareness, and contemplation before anyone enters.

▶ One at a time, each dancer enters the circle and makes a shape. The other dancers may move around the perimeter of the circle so they can look at the shape from all angles.

▶ As you feel moved, drawn, or inspired, add to the shape. You are looking at symmetrical and asymmetrical shape, lines, and energy in space, as well as the negative and positive shape the overall construction is taking.

▶ You should not censor yourself, but follow your creative, intuitive voice and keep the group shape changing.

▶ Stay in the circle and remain in your shape until you feel inclined to depart; each person should take turns in the middle. No one is to change shape inside of the circle. Each dancer will step back out to fully see what is taking place before entering again.

▶ Notice how the negative and positive spaces interact and inform each other. Notice the negative space inherent in the shapes being made, inside the curve of the arm and under the lift of the leg. Observe the whole picture.

Focal Points on the Performance Space

Focal points on the performance space are areas more readily seen by the audience. These are called *hot spots*. Focal points are more visible and have more energy in them when you are watching a dance. Think of any far back corner of the stage in comparison to the actual center of the performing space. Take a moment to imagine yourself dancing a solo on the front edge of the stage versus dancing in the back next to the curtains. You and the audience feel each other more when you are more visible to each other.

This does not mean all of the stage space is unnecessary in choreography. There are choices about where dance is happening in the space and how the location affects the overall energy and feel of the dance. When a dance is happening in a hot spot, it is saying, "Pay attention to this." When something is happening in a less conspicuous place, the choreography has more of a shadowy feel or conveys a sense of hiding or wanting to be less visible to the audience.

Exercise 10.2
Finding the Hot Spots

▶ All but three of your group members should form an audience facing an imaginary *proscenium arch*, with the remaining dancers in the stage space. Each of the remaining dancers then chooses a place on the stage and takes a neutral or pedestrian pose. They may face any direction with the intention of being seen by the audience.

▶ In the audience, discuss who is more and who is less visible, comparing each other's notes. Where are the hot spots in the performance space? How do you become more visible or less visible in the performing space?

▶ Next, the dancers should choose another place on the stage, this time with their backs to the audience. Again, the audience discusses who is more visible and why.

▶ As a dancer on the stage, you want to explore how different levels in space and how facing different directions create more or less visibility.

▶ Within your group, explore different options that have not been presented.

Defining Space

How we travel through the space and the path we travel on can be another way to show depth and cohesiveness in a dance. Shapes the dancers make as they move through space help to create flow or tension or reiterate an idea or theme in the choreography. A square says something different from a circle, a triangle, or a zigzag. A dance about the struggles of farming moving up and down the rows of the stage reinforces the concept of hardship and gives context for the viewer to connect to. For example, Helen Tamiris' dance *How Long Brethren* uses the stage space and the shapes the dancers make with their bodies to convey the hardship of sharecroppers and the unemployed in the 1930s. You create more imagery for the viewer to access by paying attention to the path the dance is taking.

Consider the vertical space as well. Today there are aerial dance companies, including Blue Lapis Light and Cirque du Soleil, where dancers perform on ribbons, ropes, and poles and down the sides of buildings.

Tamara Ashley, Choreographer

As a choreographer, I spend a great deal of time working with dancers on their inside spaces. I think it is fascinating to explore the internal architecture of the body and how working with the spaces inside can enrich and greatly inform the architectural designs of dancers moving individually and together. The short exercise below initiates an exploration into inner space:

☑ **LEARN MORE**

Scan the code or visit
http://bit.ly/AoL10tam

- Inhale and exhale, noticing the changes in your body as you breathe. The respiratory system is in constant interchange with the environment, taking in air, bringing oxygen into the circulation system so each and every cell in the body can function, and expelling waste products, such as carbon dioxide. Every moment of life is concerned with this exchange of nourishing materials and waste products, bringing the outside into our bodies and sending the inside out. Each breath changes the body by increasing and decreasing the volume of the lungs.

- Notice how, by changing your breath, you can activate physiological change. Breathe slowly and deeply, and then breathe quickly and shallowly; notice how you feel. You can literally alter the architecture of the body through breath. A dance might begin from this place. It would be a particular dance, perhaps influenced by the breath.

In fact, breath might become the organizing idea of a dance. It becomes the territory the dance inhabits and transforms space to a place. As I work on dances, I am always interested in this transformation from space to place and how the particular qualities of a dance form a territory of architectures, movement, relationships, and knowing.

What is also interesting is the exchange between inside and outside spaces and how they can often be in differential relationships. For example, after a performance, workshop, or class, I notice the internal structures of my body are still territorialized by the feeling, form, and rhythm of the phrases as I transition to my next activity. Walking down a busy London street, I notice I am not in sync with the majority of people who seem to be moving with direct purpose, eyes averted, and in haste. Having just attended to slow movement, my perception of time does not meet the particular group dynamic enacted on the street. I can choose to stay on this street or to follow another street where there are less people. If I stay on the street for a few minutes, I might start to notice I have sped up and synchronized with the group dynamic for any number of reasons – not getting in the way or being moved along by the pace of everyone else. I am now engaging in the choreography of everyday life.

You can also define space by the groupings of dancers you choreograph and how they perform the material. A corps de ballet with twenty dancers dancing in unison fills the space differently than a group of five dancers all doing their own phrase of material. When a *canon* is performed, the dancers all follow one another's movements two, four, or six counts behind, like a wave. As a result, the energy changes, and the shapes are like a crescendo in the space.

Mirroring phrases is another way to sculpt the space. When a phrase is performed with two dancers facing each other, each dancing the same material but on different sides of the body, it is as if the dance is happening in front of a mirror. Both the negative space and the positive space are then clearly defined.

Exercise 10.3
Forming Space

▶ Create a short phrase with shapes made from different body parts as your motivator. The phrase should have at least eight shapes and flow from one to the next.

▶ Teach this phrase to two or three other dancers.

▶ Collaborate and explore the different ways you can form this material, using unison movement, performing in canon, mirroring, starting at various points in the phrase, stopping and starting the phrase, including moments of stillness, or manipulating the movement in any other way you can conceive of to formulate the material and arrange the dancers.

▶ Observe how different ways of performing the movement affects the way you see the space. Record these observations in your journal.

▶ Show the study to the class and use CRP.

Creating a Spatial or Movement Score

Contemporary choreographers such as Deborah Hay create dances by formulating patterns and directions in the space for the dancers or themselves to move through. They create either a *spatial score* or a *movement score*. It defines the path the dancers will follow as they perform the prescribed vocabulary. It also provides directions and insights into the choreography and specific intentions for the vocabulary.

The spatial score and movement score can either be different or overlap. A spatial score can be just a drawing with a legend or symbols, whereas a movement score can be more elaborate. The scores enhance the idea of forming the space a step further by actually drawing out a plan and investigating the spatial patterning as an essential aspect of the choreography. Working with a score allows for a more in-depth exploration as to what the dancers' paths have to say about the specific theme or concept from which you are working.

The following is an example of a movement score. Note the detail involved, describing the movements, the dancers, the costumes, and the stage crew.

drift
by Jennifer Sherburn
Music composed by Justin Sherburn
June 2011

Drift explores "the elements" at high altitudes, including ideas I have of terrain, along with extreme weather conditions. The lives of people exposed to the environment drive the exploration.

There are five performers, forty feet by forty feet of light/neutral-toned fabric, and a pulley system. There are waist-sized holes inserted evenly throughout the fabric so all the performers can wear the fabric at once.

There are three sections.

Section One
Performers begin on stage; upstage left, completely enveloped by the fabric. There is no suggestion of human form in this moment. They slowly spread the fabric out by inching across the space, finding breath as the impetus to move, restore energy, and discover the circumstance.

Transition Between Section One and Two
They reveal themselves from the fabric being "tossed by wind/stumbling through masses of snow, unfamiliar winds, and terrain." The "wind" causes them to flip and flop, breaking away from the "ice and snow." The wind picks up speed, which results in faster, more frequent repetitions of the movement. This leads them to a more unified moment with a set sequence followed by transition to standing as well as hooking into the pulley system.

The transition to standing is forced by movement of "terrain," a type of "avalanche" that causes the performers to slip and grip and collaborate with the "force of nature" to find stable ground.

Section Two

As the performers reach stability in a standing position, the movement quiets and becomes almost still with exhaustion.

In sequence, the performers lock-in, secure themselves to each other and to the terrain, while continuing to collaborate with the movement of the fabric. (Literally, the performers hook into the pulley system and attach the fabric to their bodies. The pulley operators begin to raise the fabric to different points in space, creating a real sense of scape.)

All performers are wearing the cloth and perform a structured improvisation.

The improvisation is a response to the environment they create with the fabric.

Excerpt from the notes given to the performers:

When you move, the fabric takes on a life of its own. This is what you respond to. You are connected to each other now, but considering the circumstance of weather and ever changing terrain, you may not feel connected, maybe "numbness" and "confusion." The environment becomes unpredictable and you feel a sense of urgency for help, to communicate with someone outside of the environment. The conditions muffle any attempt, and the weather, the layers of snow filled wind, continues to disguise you.

They express this through arm gestures, level change, different configurations, and rhythms within the group. They find repetition, sequence, and rhythm. They also find absence as individuals drop due to "weakness."

Transition Between Section Two and Three

"Gust of wind" pushes/sweeps. They move in canon to create a line formation against the raised part of the fabric.

(There are two people operating the pulleys/fabric and should have it completely raised and secure by this point).

Section Three

Is slow, but repetitive with quiet, upper body movements and arm gestures. They gesture with arms to face, arms above head, and arms to embrace each other.

Overall, there is a sense of resistance, exhaustion, but with an internal eagerness to get out of the situation. Parts of them are "numb" and even more "restricted" by the weather and terrain/snow.

"The sun rises; there are radio signals coming through, but now they are snow-blind and breathless."

I would like for them, no matter how clear the movement/choreography is or how difficult the fabric is to deal with, to find constant presence and performance, filling every beat with intention and movement. I want them to strive for seamlessness no matter the vagueness of the details.

Exercise 10.4
Drawing a Spatial Score

▶ In your journal, make a map or drawing of a spatial score or movement score. Do not think too hard about what it all means. Have fun defining the space, and allow the drawing to be a creative act in itself. Think of the performing space as a place to investigate all the different angles, shapes, swirls, and hot spots. Make sure to include where the dance begins and ends and any places where the dancer may spend more or less time. Add as many details as you like, such as the type of movement happening in certain sections, the quality of the movement, the colors you see, and the feelings you have. You can use different pencil or pen colors to further define your score.

Imaginary Space

The atmosphere or the settings a dance takes place in influences the vocabulary and the character of the choreography. The *imaginary space* is where you imagine yourself being as you perform the dance. You can create the imagined space you move through as your dancing resonates from the stage. This provides the audience with a subconscious experience. The dancer's imagination transcends the performance space and helps to bring the viewer more fully into the intention of the dance.

Exercise 10.5
Using the Imaginary Space

Part One

▶ In your journal, make a list of ten environments or settings.

▶ Choose one of the settings. With two or three other dancers, imagine yourselves in that place and improvise. Tap into the sights, sounds, smells, colors, and feelings the place evokes to inspire movement. Think of gesture and how it can be abstracted. Play off of each other, responding to vocabulary, timing, rhythm, and the use of levels in space. You may choose to use words or phrases as part of the improvisation to instigate further investigation of the setting.

▶ Do the same thing with at least three other imaginary spaces. Take turns with the other dancers so all can explore something from their list.

Part Two

▶ Choose another imaginary setting or re-imagine one of the ones from before.

▶ Write down in your journal all the characteristics of this imaginary place you can think of: colors; textures; smells; tastes; kind of light; the surface of the floor/ground, walls, ceiling; sounds; presence of other people; clothing/costuming; and what it feels like to be in this space.

▶ Improvise by using five of these details, creating a movement vocabulary for each one.

▶ String the vocabulary pieces together into a series of phrases.

▶ Set this dance in the imaginary space.

▶ Decide how the dance moves through the space. The atmosphere of the imaginary place should guide you.

▶ Perform your dance as a character of this place.

▶ Break into groups and share this work with other choreographers, using the CRP method.

Conclusion

Space is a character in a dance just like a performer or a costume or a set in theatre productions. When you invest in being more conscious of what the space means to your dance, you provide an opportunity for more texture and energy to be shared with the audience.  This gives the audience more to work with, whether they know it consciously or not. Attention to the use of space also presents you with more opportunities to investigate your ideas or themes, which will in turn create more contexts for yourself.

ACC Student Case Study

Ryan Parent, Tanya Winters, and Sarah Wendtlandt

We began by visualizing a place – either imagined or an actual geographic location. We then wrote in our journals about the colors, emotions, smells, life forms, climates, and topography of our visualized location or world. We were instructed to not immediately share this information with our partners; I was paired with Gillian. We were given giving and receiving roles, which alternated and were then combined, resulting in a simultaneous exchange of giving and receiving by both partners. The informational and energetic exchanges occurred three times. Each time began with partners on opposite sides of the studio, slowly walking toward each other without dialogue, gestures, or suggestive body language, meeting in the center, rotating halfway, and then slowly walking backward in the direction of the partners' starting point.

We then wrote in our journals about our experiences, including the information we thought we had received from our partners during the transmissions. Gillian revealed to me her place was an actual geographic location: a frozen lake during the winter in Canada. She told me she felt the humans in my visualized world were floating on cloud-like structures. My world was an imagined place containing clouds of molten red lava and preceding this exercise, I had written in my journal, "Some beings don't have bodies (yet) while others (beings) dream to travel without them (their bodies)." By allowing openness and trust to inspire the way in which we gave and received information, we were able to share something intimate. To know I can have an honest, mutual openness even with a stranger or a new friend, brings me such joy and deeply connects me with the paradoxical consciousness of simultaneous oneness with individuality residing within all of us.

–Ryan

What I loved so much about the space exercise was it was simple. I just had to imagine my place and come up with phrases to describe it. I was encouraged to explore how this place made me feel. This brought me great freedom and inspiration, which helped me add the elements of time and space without feeling forced or intimidated. I was then able to understand the concepts of time, space, and descriptive phrases. This also helped me to be more open to constructive criticism from my colleagues, such as toward the definition of my world, use of focus, and eye contact.

–Tanya

I used the space exercise to help me be more aware of space and to make me travel more in my solo. In the past I would choreograph and get stuck on one side of the stage or going one direction. Having to create a fantasy space around you puts you in the world, and you can move freely in it. It opened up my spatial awareness tremendously.

Once I had my intention set and had several phrases, the next step was to expand my vocabulary. I did this several different ways. One way I expanded my vocabulary was by starting to improvise. If I liked the movement, I would repeat it to keep it in my muscle memory. Then, if the movement seemed too predictable, I would try to move to different levels, like off the ground. After coming up with new movement, I would refine it and make it my own.

Another way I expanded my movement vocabulary was to take the gestures or phrases I found most compelling and to then change them to create the same movement in a different way. There are so many ways to create but stay true to your style and main idea by just playing with it. It's like clay. Clay will always be clay, but it can be molded and reshaped however you like while always staying true to itself.

–Sarah

Outside Sources

Architecture by Frank Gehry, such as the Wiseman Art Museum, the Guggenheim Museum, and the Walt Disney Concert Hall

Architecture by Norman Foster, such as the Sage Gateshead

Helen Tamiris' *How Long Brethren*

A working score from Deborah Hay, deborahhay.com/DHDC%20Website%20Pdf/NTTF%20booklet.pdf

Eiko + Koma, eikoandkoma.org

Chapter Terms

Canon: A wave of movement in which dancers are performing the same phrase but a specific number of beats behind one another in the material.

Focal points: Points in the performing space that draw more attention.

Hot spots: Places more visible to the audience than other places on the performance space.

Imaginary space: An imagined place where the dance takes place.

Mirroring: Movement performed by two or more dancers facing each other that appears to be a mirror image.

Movement score: An elaborate map or depiction of how, why, and where a dance travels through the performing space.

Negative space: The space surrounding the shape the dancer is making.

Positive space: The physical shape the dancer makes.

Proscenium arch: The arched front opening of a traditional stage.

Spatial score: A basic map of where a dance travels through the performing space; can include drawings, text, or symbols.

Questions to Consider and Discuss

1. How do the shapes the dancers make influence the use of space in the dance?

2. How does the movement through space help to shape the architecture of the dance?

3. What are hot spots and focal points used for?

4. How do you craft the shape of the space to create more depth for the dance?

5. How can an imaginary setting help to develop a character and atmosphere for the dance?

11 ELEMENTS OF THEATRE

"To watch us dance is to hear our hearts speak."

–Hopi saying

Theatrical Elements in the Dance

Theatre and dance have always been connected. As far back as Greek theatre, dancing was integral to the overall production. For instance, in Aristophanes' play *Lysistrata*, movement is a tool to help express the message of the playwright. There is also a long history in contemporary dance of merging theatre and dance. *Dance theatre* is a popular genre that goes as far back as the beginning of the twentieth century with the Ballets Russes and Denishawn. Elements of theatre as we know it have long been present in the dances of all cultures. Costumes and *props*, for example,

In this chapter, you will explore:

- Using text in the dance

- Deciding on props and sets

- Creating lighting

- Costuming your dance

are expressive theatrical details that enhance the visual and visceral theme or context for the dance.

You can explore early modern dancers such as Mary Wigman, Martha Graham, Loie Fuller, Doris Humphrey, Katherine Dunham, and Alwin Nikolais to investigate how they incorporated theatre elements into their dances. For more contemporary works, start with the works of Pina Bausch, Elizabeth Streb, O Vertigo, La La La Human Steps, Urban Bush Women, and Big Dance Theatre.

Theatrical elements can be used as jumping-off points in your choreography, as well as tools to enhance it. You can investigate ideas and create movement by exploring different aspects of theatre.

Using Text

The use of *text* in your choreography can be an inspiration toward movement invention or can serve as an extra layer of texture in your overall dance piece. Text can be taken from a work of fiction or nonfiction, a scientific journal, poetry, or the newspaper. You can also use an original piece of writing by you, a friend, or a fellow artist. There is no one specific kind of writing more appropriate to use. Your imagination acts as a sifter, filtering through ideas and words to find what speaks or resonates with you.

Sometimes a piece of writing can be the inspiration for your dance. Sometimes it is just a place to gain ideas and investigate movement from. The text itself does not even have to be part of the finished dance. There is power in words. You can draw on the imagery, motivation, and texture and incorporate them into your choreography.

Exercise 11.1
Using Text as Movement Motivator

▶ Bring a poem or a piece of text to class.

▶ Break into duets. Take turns, with one person reading the text and the other improvising to the reading. You can explore the text more deeply by repeating words, phrases, or whole sentences. You can enhance the audio texture of the piece by changing the quality and timbre of your voice. Play with it. Imagine yourself as an actor in a play or a movie and completely invest yourself in the words.

▶ The other person dances to this soundtrack. Stay completely away from a literal interpretation or mime of the words. Let the sounds and quality of the voice inspire you. Let the images wash over you and respond to the feeling of them and not to the specific picture they create.

▶ As you take turns with this, improvise to your own and your partner's text.

▶ At the end, bring all the duets into a circle and share the reading-dancing duets with the group. Allow the group members to respond to what is authentic from their point of view. Do not judge the dances; support your fellow students in identifying what appears to be authentic movement for them.

Text as Soundscape

As you can see by the movement exploration exercise, text can be used as the music or sound to which you choreograph. A whole play or movie could be read live or recorded as the sound for your dance. Poetry can create a beautiful soundscape. For example, the words of Pablo Neruda, Maya Angelou, and Leonard Cohen are full of exquisite imagery and life. You can write your own material for your dance based on the theme you are investigating. You might also collaborate with a writer and use original text.

When you use text as your sound for a dance, you are asking the audience to listen as well as see. There is a focus on listening, as words are comprehended differently than music. There is a context you are suggesting by the choice and tone of the text. You are giving weight to a nontraditional form of accompaniment to dance. You are investigating dance and theatre together as a medium of expression.

☑ LEARN MORE

Scan the code or visit
http://bit.ly/AoL11tai

Text as Interlude

Another way to use text is as an interlude between dances. A poem or monologue can be the perfect segue or setup for a dance. You do not want to be literal with this. Check out the work of Robert Wilson and the way he uses text in his work. There is an aura of abstraction and mystery in his use of text.

It is fun to explore using text in different ways. In the end, sometimes the words become unnecessary. Sometimes they are just a way to get into what it is you are trying to say and explore.

Exercise 11.2
Using Text as Soundscape

▶ Use choreography you have already created during an exercise from a previous chapter.

▶ Find a piece of text you find inspiring. It can be read aloud or recorded. Use this as the sound for your existing choreography.

▶ Explore the movement using the tone, rhythm, and essence of the words to influence how the dance is performed. See how you can play with the timing of the dance in relationship to the reading. Improvise with the material and the text until you find a combination that speaks to you.

Creating a Set

A *set* for a dance is a staged environment the dancers move through or with. Often the setting symbolizes an idea or theme for the dance. Sometimes there is no relationship whatsoever, as in choreographer Merce Cunningham's *RainForest*, which used silver pillows, created by visual artist Andy Warhol, hanging and floating in the stage area. Many story ballets and contemporary companies' works have elaborate sets.

A set can be as simple as a video projection or a series of objects placed around the stage. Choreographers have used benches, sofas, tables, chairs, door frames, windows, fences, whole living rooms, and pretty much anything else you can imagine. A set adds concreteness to the dance. There is a weight to the idea or symbol of what the set represents. Choreography becomes a language imbued in the landscape of the stage. There is a dialogue between the movement and the set. The set can be danced on, with, through, or ignored. Collaborations with visual artists are customary reltionships for dance makers wishing to include a set in their work. Just as a set designer can do for a play, another artist can inspire awareness of and add depth to the choreographer's idea or theme.

Exercise 11.3
Visualizing a Set

▶ In your journal, make a list of ten set ideas. Allow yourself to imagine far and wide.

▶ Pick one of these ideas and write about it. Include color, texture, surface area, dimensions, and as many details as you can imagine.

▶ Write down the kinds of dance that happen in this space. What is the theme or driving force of the dance? What qualities does the movement have? How many dancers are there? Is there text? What do the costumes look like?

Props

A prop is an object you dance with or use in the course of a dance. It is meant to express some component of the theme of the work. Using a prop helps to create symbolism on the performance space and adds dimension to the dance. It can also be distracting. It is important to know why you are introducing something, besides the dancer's body, onto the stage; you must have a reason in mind for including a prop in a dance.

A prop can be anything you can carry or move around with. Kitchenware, toiletries, food, flowers, balls of all sizes, ropes, scarves, yards of fabric – just about anything you come up with can be a prop. Choreographer Loie Fuller often used many yards of silk fabric as her costume, prop, and set. Choreographer Jessica Lindberg Coxe's reconstruction of Fuller's *Fire Dance* is an amazing example of how a dance is made with a dancer manipulating something besides her body.

147

Exercise 11.4
Exploring an Object

▶ Pick an object from your home.

▶ Improvise with the object, letting it direct the movement. Do this in a literal way, using the object as you would in real life.

▶ Improvise with the object in an abstract way, allowing it to become many things at once.

▶ Improvise as if your body is the prop, without using the object. Do you need the prop, or is it just a jumping-off point for you to create material?

▶ Create a study combining material from all three ways of improvising with the prop.

▶ Break into groups and share this work with other choreographers, using the CRP method.

Using Light

Good lighting for a dance is a character in itself. If you are presenting a dance onstage, it is important for the dancer to be seen. There are many ways to manipulate light. It is important for you as the choreographer to have an idea of how light can work in your dance. Lighting designers are dancers' best friends when a dance is performed in a theatrical setting.

You can highlight a dancer or dancers by setting them apart on the performance space from other dancers. You can use pools of light to isolate and highlight a performer, as in David Parson's dance *Caught*. *Light as character* is another theatrical element. The use of shadows behind the dancers on a *cyclorama* can be an ominous character.

The color of the light is also a tool to accentuate your choreography. Different saturations of color are added to the front of a lighting instrument by using *gels*. Next time you are at a performance of any kind, whether it is a music concert, dance, or play, notice how the lighting plays a significant role in the overall look of the stage. Notice what colors are used where and how that affects your feelings about what is going on.

Ruth Grauert, Choreographer

Someone I find very inspiring is Alwin Nikolais (1910-1993). Nikolais employed dance as the core of his theatre of light, sound, and motion. He created many multimedia works for his internationally acclaimed company, The Nikolais Dance Theatre. His use of lighting, costumes, and properties was groundbreaking, exploring a wide variety of approaches and techniques. Nikolais made dances with light (flashlights, streaks of light, projected patterns), dances with stuff (sticks and cones, barrels, and mirrors), and dances with "made-up" costumes (sacks, wigs and masks).

☑ LEARN MORE

Scan the code or visit
http://bit.ly/AoL11gra

Costuming

Costuming is another theatrical element of choreography. What a dancer wears in a dance is important to how the dance is viewed. A costume can be a neutral statement or a suggestive one. What you choose to wear in a dance provides an opportunity to enhance the overall theme of the work.

Exercise 11.5
Starting with a Costume

▶ Find an outfit or clothing you find inspiring or sparks an idea for a dance.

▶ Put the costume on and start exploring the movement it suggests to you. Improvise with the idea in mind of where you might wear this costume. What would be the imaginary setting or set in which you are dancing?

▶ What kind of music or sound does this costume suggest? Improvise with that in mind.

▶ Come up with a structured improvisation based on these explorations. It does not have to be a set of phrases, but it can be a loosely structured set of movement ideas and points in space you connect to as you are dancing.

Choices of fabric and color help to define the costume. Whether the fabric is stiff or flowing suggests ideas to the audience. Pedestrian wear – such as jeans, shorts, or suits – may indicate a setting or theme. Bathing suits indicate water is nearby, just as ball gowns indicate a formal dance or fancy party. The important thing to consider is whether a costume is appropriate for the dance and the audience. Having a lot of bare skin exposed for no other reason besides you think you look good is not really a costuming choice. You want to think about your dance and have the costume be an integral element of the concept.

Costume designers for dance are an amazing breed of artists. They understand movement and also have the ability to incorporate theme and concept into their work. It is a fun collaboration to have a costume designer working with you on your dance. Providing an image or place to start from allows the designer to run in many directions but still stay close to your concept for your choreography.

Exercise 11.6
Bringing it Together

▶ Start with your movement and text from Exercise 11.1.

▶ Find a prop that will enliven this material. Explore the movement using the prop.

▶ Choose a setting for this dance. Create it simply or just imagine it in the space. Keep exploring, using all of these elements together.

▶ Think of a costume to go with this material. Play with the costume in relationship to the rest of the elements.

▶ Put together a small dance from all of this material. You may choose whether or not to incorporate the prop(s) or the set pieces.

Conclusion

Including text, props, and some sort of set in your work is an individual choice. It is fun to explore all of these theatrical elements, and it is good to add these things to your toolbox in order to play and investigate with different ways to get into a dance. Maybe you are walking down the street and you see the light hit a tree in a certain way, and the moment inspires a dance in you. Remember, there is no right or wrong way to find your way into a dance.

Elements of theatre are an inherent part of a completed choreographic vision. However, you will not always have your dances produced on a stage with lighting, a set, and ornate costumes. Thinking about these things, though, can help to inform you, guide you, and inspire you in your dance-making process. Keep in mind that costuming will almost always play a part in one way or another. After all, whether you are performing on a stage, outside in a park, or in an informal studio setting, you need to be wearing something!

ACC Student Case Study

Atticus Prime and Yvonne Keyrouz

Text is a meaningful way to describe dance intention. Various artists use it in different ways, whether it's mounted on a projector screen or relayed in the back of a musical score. Sometimes it's just plain read. Regardless of how it is used, when you dance to it, never dance to the words, but to the intention of what the words mean. For example, if the text mentions certain body parts, don't stand up and point to the certain parts of the body. Maybe do a sequence of movements to captivate the use of those body parts.

Improvisation to text should not be a difficult thing, especially if the dancer feels and understands the meaning of the words. Personally, I think people get confused about improvisational dancing because they think, "Oh it's something right on the spot I have to do every time." A handy tip towards this style of dance is setting up a little bit of vocabulary. Then, when performing the improvisation, it looks more professional and doesn't have the feeling of "Um, what am I going to do next?" This will particularly help you not feel like you have to translate the meaning of the text directly in your dance, but it will allow you to be free to express yourself.

–Atticus

I found that really exploring the props helped me feel more comfortable using them and revealed more possibilities regarding ways to use them in a dance. I began working with newspapers and started with three ideas, each exploring a different use of the newspapers.

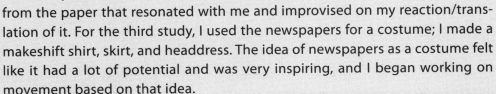

The first study involved using the papers as a surface to tap on. For the second study, I picked a story from the paper that resonated with me and improvised on my reaction/translation of it. For the third study, I used the newspapers for a costume; I made a makeshift shirt, skirt, and headdress. The idea of newspapers as a costume felt like it had a lot of potential and was very inspiring, and I began working on movement based on that idea.

In spite of the initial inspiration, though, I had a hard time coming up with anything else until I really knew what my dance was about. I sat down and thought about the newspapers, their purpose, and what they hold. I realized that newspapers serve to communicate and connect people all over the world.

nect people all over the world. Each story affects the reader in some way, and everything that happens in the world touches us in some way.

So I decided to pick three stories from a paper that impacted me personally, and instead of starting my dance in a costume made out of newspapers, I would let the papers stick to me as I danced, illustrating the idea that we are affected by people's stories. I shredded about ten newspapers into varying sizes of strips and sections to cover the floor with and wrapped sections of my arms, legs, and waist with double sided packing tape, making it possible for the papers to stick to me every time I went to the floor in my dance.

–Yvonne

Outside Sources

Historical videos of modern dance pioneers

Martha Graham's *Lamentation*

Loie Fuller's *Fire Dance*, reconstructed by Jessica Lindberg Coxe

Contemporary choreography listed throughout the chapter, which can be found on YouTube and other websites

Poets Mary Oliver, Maya Angelou, e. e. cummings, Theodore Roethke, Pablo Neruda, Leonard Cohen, and many more for text for your dances

Fashion ads, magazines, and people on the street for costume ideas

The changing light on a sunny day and a cloudy day, for ideas about lighting, color, and mood

Plays and other performances, to investigate theatrical elements

Chapter Terms

Costuming: Clothing the dancer(s) wear to fit the choreography and theme of the dance.

Cyclorama: A large white screen at the back of a stage onto which light and images can be projected.

Dance theatre: A term used to describe a dance work that includes theatrical elements.

Gel: A thin sheet of polycarbonate or polyester material that is placed in front of a lighting instrument that provides colored light for the stage.

Light as character: Using light as a theatrical element in a dance.

Props: Objects that inspire the dance or become part of the choreography.

Set: The environment in which a dance is set; a theatrical space created for a dance to take place.

Text: Writing used in your choreography as either a soundtrack or an inspiration for movement vocabulary.

Theatre: An artistic expression that can include a script, acting, dancing, costumes, light, set, props, video, or other technology and usually portrays a story.

Questions to Consider and Discuss

1. How are theatre and dance connected?

2. How can the use of text inform your choreography?

3. What theatrical elements are you attracted to? Why?

4. How does lighting become a character in the dance?

5. How can costuming add to or subtract from the impact of the dance?

6. How would you define a dance theatre work in comparison with a regular dance piece?

12 REHEARSAL AND PERFORMANCE

"So, I think I would say, enjoy the process of learning to dance. The process of our profession, and not its final achievement, is the heart and soul of dance."

—Jacques d'Amboise

Where have you been? Where are you going?

Making a dance is such a glorious task. Not only can it teach you how to be creative and express yourself, but it can also teach you life lessons. Through the choreographic process, you can come up against your insecurities and the nagging voices telling you something is not good enough, you are not talented enough, or you do not have any ideas. None of those voices speak the truth. Creativity and dance-making are

In this chapter, you will explore:

- Planning a rehearsal

- Using proper rehearsal etiquette

- Preparing for a performance

- Using proper performance etiquette

processes you learn by following through with the action, by doing, and by making choices.

There is a lot to be learned in the *rehearsal process* and in the *performance process*. Both require planning, scheduling, and staying on task. Both require the kind of focus you can use in all areas of your life. Staying on task is no small feat. Following through as you enter into the unknown and try to find the other side can be scary and exhilarating. As you begin rehearsing and performing your choreography, there are some things to understand and become familiar with.

Rehearsal Process

Casting is an important aspect of making a dance. You want to know how many dancers fit into your vision and cast accordingly. However, you might have to rethink your vision depending on the dancers who are available. Being flexible is important because dancers get hurt and cannot rehearse or perform all the time; they may get sick or travel.

Once you know who is in your cast, it is time to set a rehearsal schedule. Give yourself plenty of time to rehearse in order to take the pressure off of both you and the dancers. Rehearsal is more fun when everyone is working and relaxed and not always feeling the pressure of perfecting the material and performance.

Kathy Dunn Hamrick, Choreographer

When you work collaboratively like we (as choreographers) do, it's important to know when to talk and when to listen, when to direct and when to step back. A typical Kathy Dunn Hamrick Dance Company (KDH) rehearsal begins with my stating the goals for the particular day. I then follow up by asking the dancers what they need in order for us to move forward together and achieve those goals.

Because I hire dancers who want to invest themselves in the work, to be included in the process, and to problem-solve on their own, I bring in plenty of prepared material, but I also reserve space and time for the dancers to play. This not only allows for wonderful accidents to happen, but it also provides a sense of ownership on the part of the dancers.

No matter how many times I watch the company onstage, performances are still magical. With each show, I find new moments of power as the dancers continually invest themselves in the movement and in each other. Before we leave for the night, these are the things I share with the dancers as they sit quietly in the performance space.

☑ **LEARN MORE**

Scan the code or visit
http://bit.ly/AoL12kdh

Time should be included in the rehearsal process for exploring and improvising. It is good to start with movement material and an idea or theme, but sometimes in the rehearsal process your ideas change and morph. This is good. Allowing the dance to have a life of its own is necessary. The creative process is a living one, and it requires you to listen and learn to recognize when to let go of something that is not working or speaking to you any longer. There has to be room in the rehearsal process for your intuition to be heard.

Setting a Rehearsal Schedule

Setting a schedule that fits the availability of all dancers is important so you can make the most of each rehearsal. It is harder to work when only half of your cast is present. You must get a commitment from the dancers for a rehearsal schedule. You all have other obligations, so it is important to be direct in asking for all involved to be realistic about when and how much time they have. It gets frustrating very quickly when people cannot make rehearsals because they have not managed their time effectively.

Exercise 12.1
Planning and Scheduling a Rehearsal

▶ Use an exercise from a previous chapter you feel may extend into a full dance. Using a calendar, set an imaginary performance date two months out. Think about approximately how long this dance will be. How many times a week will you need to rehearse and for how long to accomplish the goal of finishing the dance before the performance? Here is a helpful tip for you: It is best to finish the dance a few rehearsals before the performance so the dancers have time to embody the dance and you have time to *clean* it.

▶ Write out your schedule. Allow at least twenty minutes for a warm-up and to meet with your cast for notes and questions at the beginning of your rehearsals. You will need approximately one hour to develop or set thirty seconds of choreography. A five-minute dance will need at least ten rehearsal hours plus three to four hours of warm-up time and notes. If you are very efficient, you'll need thirteen to fourteen hours of rehearsal time to build the dance and at least two one-hour rehearsals to prepare the work for performance.

▶ So far, you have a total of fifteen rehearsals, which, spread out over a two-month period, will mean seven or eight rehearsals the first month and seven or eight rehearsals the second month. With four weeks in a month, you will need to plan at least two one-hour rehearsals per week for both months. This is a very minimal schedule, and to really take the time to explore and develop your work, you might need to double this time frame. If the work will be performed in a traditional stage setting, you will need additional time for technical and dress rehearsals.

▶ Now create a plan for each rehearsal of what you will be working on and exploring during that time. Realize your plan more than likely will change or even get thrown out the window. Even so, having a plan ensures you will know how to get started even if you do not feel particularly inspired that day. Know what you want to accomplish, whether it is a chunk of time you are looking to fill or a phrase or section you want to perfect.

▶ Remember your dance is your own process. Your first rehearsal may be working out the ending, investigating a theme or set of movements, or just seeing how the different dancers in your cast move. Build in time for exploration and improvisation.

Rehearsal Etiquette

As the choreographer, you have to set the standard for what is acceptable *rehearsal etiquette*. This is not to say you should behave like an army general, but there are a few guidelines to understand and follow. It is your job to set these guidelines and make it clear you expect everyone to follow them.

Being respectful of others' time, talent, and willingness to be part of your work and being considerate are mandatory if you want to maintain an open and happy working environment. There is no reason to treat people any other way. Check your attitude at the door. If you become frustrated in a rehearsal, maybe you are not being clear enough about what you are asking of the dancers. Move on to plan B and try explaining things in another way.

As an alternative, have the dancers ask you questions about what they are doing or not understanding, so you can get a clear idea about their concerns and challenges. They may all be struggling with the same movement. By asking them directly, you know to work on improving a particular issue rather than spending time on an entire section or the whole dance.

Start and Finish Time

It is extremely important you adhere to the start and finish times for rehearsals. Therefore, you as the choreographer must be on time. If you start coming late, everyone else will start to follow your example. Finishing on time is important because everyone has busy lives; most dancers have to go to work, go to class, study, or babysit siblings and cannot hang around just because you get inspired five minutes before rehearsal ends. You can always ask people if they can stay a bit longer, but do not expect it. Avoid doing vital work if only some dancers can stay longer.

Exercise 12.2
Making a Dance

▶ You have worked out how to schedule a rehearsal and the elements you need for the rehearsal process. Throughout this book, you have done many exercises and explored a plethora of choreographic concepts. These exercises are all just beginnings, places to start, and examples of how to begin the process of actually crafting a dance.

▶ Go back through the exercises in your journal and the notes you made about your movements and start working. Look back through the chapters and reacquaint yourself with the various examples of how to explore the concepts.

▶ Reread what other choreographers and student choreographers did and used, and what they think about in their choreographic process. Feel free to borrow ideas from any of them. Take a risk and explore your own intuitive notions. Go online and watch more dances, read choreography books, and, most importantly, go see a dance and start noticing what really speaks to you.

▶ Now, make a dance! Remember it's your process and your dance. Enjoy the art of listening.

Choreographers have rehearsal plans. You show up at rehearsal prepared and ready to work. A little chitchat in the beginning of rehearsal to break the ice and get relaxed is fine. Remember, though, time is finite, and you are there for a purpose. Having a plan enables you to jump right in and get moving. There is nothing worse for dancers than standing around. They want to dance, move, and be creative. It is your job as the choreographer to figure out how to keep them motivated. Happy dancers are sweaty dancers who feel they have worked hard and have accomplished something.

Being Flexible

Remember to be flexible with your plan. Dancers have crises – life sometimes gets in the way of art. Be ready to change your plan if necessary. You may need to find a new dancer, scale back, or give another dancer a bigger role than you had anticipated. Change is the only constant in life, and embodying change in your art is what makes your art authentic and accessible.

Exercise 12.3
Following CRP

▶ It is time to use the CRP to help you through the creation of a dance. Set a schedule of showings and form a group to support you and your choreographic vision. You can use the CRP with the whole class or with a smaller group of choreographers. Allow a set period of time for each choreographer to share work and receive feedback.

▶ Take notes as you watch others' work and be prepared with your own questions about your work. Remember to be neutral in your questions as the goal is to help each other make the dance the way the choreographer is envisioning and not the dance you want them to make.

▶ Set the schedule to allow ample time between showings for you to ponder the information given and incorporate the feedback you received and the knowledge you gained through the process.

Remember, your dancers can provide you with inspiration, feedback, and ideas. Learn how to listen to them, but also know where you are going. Do not feel obliged to follow somebody else's good idea. Watch how the dancers perform your material. You might want to incorporate some of their idiosyncrasies. Letting the dancers improvise with your material is also a great way to investigate what you are doing. Creating a set of challenges for the dancers to manipulate the choreography is another way to gain insight into your work and see it from another perspective.

Performance Process

The performance process differs from the rehearsal process in that you are now moving toward the presentation of your work for an audience. There are specific details to pay attention to in this process. It is your job as the choreographer to be aware of them and to make your dancers aware of them so they can do the best job possible of performing your work.

Knowing the Performance Space

First, you want to make sure the dance you have choreographed in rehearsal will fit into the performance space. It is not often you rehearse in the same size space as the performance space. As you can imagine, a different-sized space can have quite a different impact on a dance. You need to check the *spacing* for your dance to fit it on the stage. You can do this with a tape measure in rehearsal. Acquire the dimensions of the stage and mark it off in the rehearsal space. If you are lucky, you can

have a *spacing rehearsal* on the stage, fitting the dance to your actual performance space. Either way, you want to make sure the dance fits the stage and you have time to make any necessary adjustments so the dancers feel comfortable with what they are doing.

You also want to check where the *wings* are for a

dancer's *entrance* onto and *exit* off of the performance space. If your dance has dancers going on and off of the stage, you want to make sure they practice those entrances and exits; the movements must be done cleanly.

If you are performing on a traditional proscenium stage, there may be lighting instruments in the wings. This equipment can be on the floor or on poles in the middle of the wings. The lighting instruments on the floor are known as *shin busters* because that is exactly what it feels like if you run into one of them as you exit the stage.

You will also have to consider *sight lines*, which in a traditional stage are the spaces in the wings where the audience can see the performer as he or she is waiting to go on. It is unprofessional to be seen in the wings. You do not want to distract the audience from what is happening on the performance space by calling attention to the wing space. Sight lines differ from theatre to theatre, but a basic rule of thumb is this: If you can see the audience, the audience can see you. While you are waiting in the wings, be quiet and respectful of the dancing onstage. Your energy should be tuned to watching for your entrance and supporting the performers.

Of course, you could be performing your work in a more informal studio setting. Setting up spacing and understanding your entrances and exits still pertain in this kind of setting. It is even more important, though, for you to be still and attentive when you are totally visible standing on the side and waiting to enter the dance. Do not pull focus from the dance by fidgeting. Give your attention to your fellow dancers and be present in the space.

BACKSTAGE

SHIN BUSTER

Technical Rehearsals

If you are performing in a traditional theatre space, you will more than likely have some sort of *technical rehearsal*. Technical rehearsals are important because they give everyone an opportunity to practice their part in the production in conjunction with everyone else.

You and the dancers may have been practicing for months, but it is highly unlikely you have been practicing on the stage. A technical rehearsal will help the dancers become comfortable working in the performance space. This is also your opportunity to get to know the various backstage personnel. The technical crew will probably be seeing the dance for the first time and receiving their *cues*, which tell them when to turn the music and lights on or when to change lights or close the curtains.

The technical crew consists of the people who support your dance by running the sound, lights, and curtains. The *crew* includes a *stage manager*, *lighting designer*, *light board operator*, *sound board operator*, and a variety of *stagehands*. The stagehands pull curtains and help to place and remove props from the stage. The stage manager directs the show, calls the cues, and guides all of the backstage activity. The lighting designer creates the light for your dance. The light board operator follows the directions of the stage manager and runs the lights cues. The sound board operator also follows the directions of the stage manager and makes sure your sound comes on and goes off at the appropriate time. All of these people work to make you and your dance look and sound as good as possible. It is essential for you to be clear and polite with all of them. They will respect your work more if you respect theirs.

As the choreographer, you want to be able to articulate the details of how the dance should be presented. If you have ideas for what you want the lights to look like, it is appropriate to share them with the lighting designer. You will need your costumes for the technical rehearsals. The lighting designer must see the costumes on your dancers as they move in the space to provide the best light and color choices for your work. Your music should be on a separate CD or other medium as requested by the theatre. Only your music for your dance should be on the CD. The sound board operator cannot search through tracks during a performance.

Dress Rehearsal

The *dress rehearsal* is the true practice for the performance. Everyone involved gets a chance to make sure they are doing their jobs as if they were in front of an audience. You want to be thoroughly warmed up. Your makeup and hair should be just like you are going to have it for the actual performance. Whatever you need to be wearing under your costume should be worn. You should present yourself and perform as if you are in front of an audience. The dress rehearsal is your final chance to catch problems with any of the elements prior to the performance.

Performance Etiquette

The day of the show is as important as the show itself. You want to conserve your energy for the show and not waste it running around needlessly. Your focus for the day should be on your performance as much as possible.

Performance etiquette requires you have a good class to warm you up before the show. When you are backstage waiting for your performance, you must spend the time staying warm and focusing on your role in the show. Put your electronic devices away and stay connected to your dancing and the other dancers. Backstage and in the dressing area is not the place to be talking or texting on your cellphone. Being centered and quiet will ensure you do a good job in the performance. Create rituals to center yourself. Make cards for or give small gifts to your dancers to encourage them and to thank them for being a part of your work. Have enough water and simple snacks to keep everyone going.

The Bow

The last thing the audience sees of your work is the *bow*. Make sure it is clean and simple. Remember the audience is there to see you and support you. Be gracious and open to applause. You have worked hard to get to the stage and perform your work. You have just shared and expressed something uniquely yours. Enjoy the moment as the lights go out and the dance is over.

Conclusion

The rehearsal process is an important element of your choreography. While planning the rehearsal, you must choose your cast and develop a flexible schedule around your cast's availabilities. As the choreographer, you have to set the standard of the rehearsal etiquette. Be on time, be respectful, and be kind to your cast. Be mindful of staying on time and on track.

The performance process is the final step of your choreography. Become familiar with the performance space and make sure the dance will fit in the available space. Have a technical rehearsal so your crew – stage manager, lighting designer, and stagehands, for instance – will know how things will work on the performance day. A dress rehearsal will help everyone get a feel of what the final performance will be like, from the costuming to the makeup.

ACC Student Case Study

Lindsay Robinson

As you already know, processes grow, change, and develop from dance to dance. There are, however, some common practices I have learned and almost always use when beginning to work on a dance. I do my best to come to rehearsals with a list of things to work on. The ideas I bring range from a concept to a mood to a story to actual movements. I try to come with more than enough material to keep us working for the duration of the rehearsal and then some. Having plenty of ideas helps to sooth the awkwardness of a first rehearsal. When the dancer(s) and I first step foot into a rehearsal space, I like to clarify that choreography is a patient process and we are going to try out some ideas and movements. Some of these ideas and movements may hang around for further development, and others may disappear. Be open.

I like to begin moving in an improvisational fashion in the beginning. I improvise using words that deal with the mood I want to create at a particular moment, are related to the theme I want to convey, or are unrelated to what I feel like creating. An improvisation session allows me to see how the dancers move and also highlights their strengths and common movement patterns. Eventually, as partnering begins, it allows me to see how the dancers interact and move together. I remind the dancers to repeat any movements that speak to them or feel good when they do them. I also take note of any "aha" moments.

I have come to learn I am a big fan of gestural movement. I feel gestures are often common actions relatable to both the dancer and the audience. There is already a basic movement to play with when dealing with gestures. Gestures are a good starting place for me.

As music is added to the work in progress, I make a musical map of the song. I sit and note times of future or current music cues. Additionally, I am able to better understand the course of the dance. For example, when Headlong Dance

Theater came to ACC about two years ago, they had us create a mini combination. While performing the same dance, Andrew, of Headlong, would change the music after each run. I realized how much music can affect and alter the entire mood of the dance. I think about this and often use this method of trying different songs to create a dance.

I also enjoy using imagery. Photos, paintings, and artwork of any kind can serve as inspiration for movement and ideas to form the dance. I also draw pictures of the dance as it progresses. I use these drawings when I have a particular movement I want to try, when I want to remember a movement sequence, or when I want to draw floor patterns. One thing I would like to do more is jot down my thoughts before and/or after a rehearsal. I feel doing this would help me better understand my process as well as progress the work to performance-ready status.

I am learning more and more about choreography all the time. Being open and having a willingness to try and play with movement are essential to the choreographic process. Standing still thinking should only last in minimal spurts. "When in doubt, keep moving" is one of my mottos. Embracing the moments when I wonder why I am a dancer only makes me stronger when I continue and do not give up on myself. There is always inspiration waiting for me to remind me why I dance.

Outside Sources

☑ **LEARN MORE**

Scan the code or visit
http://bit.ly/AoL12mg

Dv8: Physical Theatre. DVD. Directed by David Hinton and Clara van Gool. Berlin, Germany: Arthaus Musik, 2007

Minton, Sandra Cerny. *Choreography: A Basic Approach Using Improvisation*. 3rd ed. Illinois: Human Kinetics Publishers, 2007

Martha Graham. *Martha Graham - Dance On Film*. Directed by Nathan Kroll. New York: Criterion Collection, 2007

Chapter Terms

Bow: The last thing the audience sees of your work; your way of thanking the audience.

Clean: To make the dance performance ready.

Crew: People who work a show.

Cues: The prompts telling a crew member what to do and when.

Dress rehearsal: A true practice of a performance with all of the elements: the dance, sound, lighting, costumes, and makeup.

Entrance: When a dancer enters into the dance.

Exit: When a dancer leaves the dance.

Light board operator: Person who runs the lights for a show.

Lighting designer: Person who designs lighting for performances.

Performance etiquette: Positive code of behavior to ensure a performance runs smoothly.

Performance process: The process of readying a dance for performance.

Rehearsal etiquette: Positive code of behavior to ensure a rehearsal runs smoothly.

Rehearsal process: The process of organizing and running a rehearsal.

Shin busters: Lighting instruments sitting on the floor in the wings.

Sight lines: Space in the wings where a performer can be seen.

Sound board operator: Person who runs the sound for a show.

Spacing: Making a dance fit a performance space.

Spacing rehearsal: Rehearsal in the performance space that fits the dance to the space.

Stagehands: People in the backstage area who support the performance and performers.

Stage manager: Person who is in charge of the support crew.

Technical rehearsal: Rehearsal where all involved in the performance figure out their roles.

Wings: Curtains at the side of the stage where the dancers enter and exit.

Questions to Consider and Discuss

1. What is the importance of understanding the rehearsal process?

2. What are the elements of a good rehearsal?

3. What is the dancer's role in the rehearsal process?

4. What is the choreographer's role in the rehearsal process?

5. How are the rehearsal process and the performance process different?

6. How do following rehearsal and performance etiquettes enhance these processes?

7. Performing onstage is not just about the dancer. Explain the importance of the collaborative process with all the players involved: stagehands, lighting designer, stage manager, and other performers.

8. What is the purpose of the technical rehearsal?

9. What is the importance of the dress rehearsal?

10. What kind of performance rituals can you create for yourself?

BIBLIOGRAPHY

American Masters. "Merce Cunningham: A Lifetime of Dance." www.pbs.org/wnet/americanmasters/episodes/merce-cunningham/a-lifetime-of-dance/566.

Art in Sight. "Abstract Expressionism." bsu.edu/artinsight/Timeline/timeline_abstract_expressionism.html.

Au, Susan. *Ballet and Modern Dance*. London: Thames and Hudson Publishers, 2002.

Bales, Melanie and Rebecca Nettl-Fiol, eds. *The Body Eclectic: Evolving Practices in Dance Training*. Champaign, IL: University of Illinois Press, 2008.

Banes, Sally. *Terpsichore in Sneakers: Post-Modern Dance*, 1st Edition. Middleton, CT: Wesleyan University Press, 1987.

Bill T. Jones/Arnie Zane Dance Company. "Company History and Mission Statement." www.billtjones.org/about_us/company_history.php.

Brehm, Mary Ann and Lynne McNett. *Creative Dance for Learning: The Kinesthetic Link*. Columbus, OH: McGraw-Hill, 2007.

CKUIK. "Meredith Monk YouTube Videos." www.ckuik.com/Meredith_Monk.

Conditioning for Dance: Training for Peak Performance in All Dance Forms. Champaign, IL: Human Kinetics, 2003.

Contact Quarterly. "CQ's Contact Improvisation Resource Page." www.contactquarterly.com/cq/webtext/resource.html.

Dali Lama and Howard C. Cutler. *The Art of Happiness: A Handbook for Living*. London: Hodder and Stoughton, 1998.

Fitt, Sally S. *Dance Kinesiology*. New York: Schirmer Books, 1996.

Fraleigh, Sondra Horton. *Dancing into Darkness: Butoh, Zen, and Japan*. Pittsburgh: University of Pittsburgh Press, 1999.

Hay, Deborah. *My Body, The Buddhist*. Middleton, CT: Wesleyan University Press, 2000.

Headlong Dance Theater. "Company." www.headlong.org/company.html.

Kapit, Wynn. *Anatomy Coloring Book*. San Francisco: Benjamin Cummings, 2001.

Lerman, Liz and John Borstel. *Liz Lerman's Critical Response Process: A Method of Getting Useful Feedback on Anything You Make, from Dance to Dessert*. Takoma Park, MD: Liz Lerman Dance Exchange, 2003.

McGraw-Hill Higher Education. "Lynne McNett." www.mhprofessional.com/mhhe_contributor.php?id=30536.

McGraw-Hill Higher Education. "Mary Ann Brehm." www.mhprofessional.com/mhhe_contributor.php?id=50811.

Merce Cunningham Dance Company. "Artistic Advisors." www.merce.org/company/artists.php.

Merriam-Webster Editorial Staff. *Merriam Webster's Collegiate Dictionary:* 11th Edition. Springfield, MA: Merriam-Webster, Inc., 2008.

Moore, Thomas. *Care of the Soul: A Guide for Cultivating Depth and Sacredness in Everyday Life*. New York: HarperPerennial, 1994.

Morgenroth, Joyce. *Dance Improvisations*. Pittsburgh: University of Pittsburgh Press, 1987.

MusicWeb International. "Mark Morris's Guide to Twentieth Century Composers." www.musicweb-international.com/Mark_Morris/index.htm.

National Public Radio. "Merce Cunningham: Dance at the Edge." www.npr.org/templates/story/story.php?storyId=6692356.

Pan's Labyrinth. "Guillermo del Toro's Sketchbook." www.panslabyrinth.com/sketchbook.html.

Sans Souci Festival of Dance. Last modified 2011. www.sanssoucifest.org.

Schwartz, Peggy and Murray Schwartz. *The Dance Claimed Me: A Biography of Pearl Primus*. New Haven: Yale University Press, 2011.

Strosnider, Luke. "ART: 'Inspired by Music'." *Rochester City Newspaper*. www.rochestercitynewspaper.com/entertainment/art ART:++Inspired+by+Music+.

University of Frankfurt. "Introduction to Labanotation." user.uni-frankfurt.de/~griesbec/LABANE.HTML.

"What inspires the inspirational: Icons of art, science and politics give us their answers." *The Independent*. May 22, 2006. www.independent.co.uk/news/media/what-inspires-the-inspirational-icons-of-art-science-and-poltics-give-us-their-answers-479170.html.

CONTRIBUTOR BIOGRAPHIES

Tamara Ashley is an artist and scholar who has worked across a broad range of professional, educational, and community contexts to get people dancing and moving in the studio, in the theatre, and in the outdoors (a particular passion). She holds a PhD in Ecological Choreographic Practices from Texas Woman's University. Her work has been supported by several grants from the Arts Council England. She is currently a Senior Lecturer in Dance at the University of Bedfordshire, where she directs the Master of Arts degree in Choreography and Performance. She is also the artistic director of DanceDigital. From 2002 to 2010, she held a senior lectureship at Northumbria University, where she led the Bachelor of Arts Dance Choreography program, a joint initiative between Dance City and Northumbria University. While at Northumbria, she received a research informed teaching award and two applauding and promoting teaching awards.

Mary Ann Brehm has a PhD in Dance from the University of Wisconsin at Madison. She taught dance at the University of Wisconsin at Whitewater, University of Wisconsin at Madison, and the University of Vermont. She was a member of the Barbara Mettler Dance Company and has served on the Board of Directors for The International Association for Creative Dance. She has been integrating dance with school curricula for many years and has won several awards for her arts education programs, including the Tucson Unified School District's Opening Minds through the Arts Program and the University of Arizona's Project DISCOVER. She also has written several publications exploring the use of dance for educational purposes, including building communities and promoting individual growth.

José Luis Bustamante is the Dance Department Chair at Austin Community College. He is the former artistic director of Sharir + Bustamante Danceworks, and his work has been commissioned by such organizations as Ballet Austin, Cleveland's Repertory Project, Florida State University, and the University of Texas at Austin. He received Choreographer Fellowships from the National Endowment for the Arts in 1993, 1994, and 1995. Bustamante is also an alumnus of The Yard in Martha's Vineyard, Massachusetts. In addition, he has taught for Dance Alloy in Pittsburgh, Pennsylvania, and Cleveland State University and served as a panelist for the National Endowment for the Arts and Dance Advance. Originally from Mexico, Bustamante received a Bachelor of Fine Arts degree in Communication Sciences from the Instituto Tecnológico y de Estudios Superiores de Monterrey and holds an MFA in Dance from Hollins University/American Dance Festival.

Ana Baer Carrillo has been nationally and internationally active as a choreographer and video-artist since 1992. In 2003, she co-founded Avant Media Performance with composer Randy Gibson. Since 2005, she has been the artistic co-director of Sans Souci Festival of Dance Cinema, along with Michelle Ellsworth. In 2009, she founded Bitcho

Maria Productions with video artist Caren McCaleb. Her body of work – consisting of video dance, video installation, interdisciplinary performances, and choreography – has been produced in Germany, France, Greece, Mexico, and venues throughout the United States. She holds a Licentiate of Choreography from the Centro Nacional de las Artes in Mexico City as well as a Full Teaching Certificate from the Royal Academy of Dance. In 2000, she moved from Mexico to the United States and attended the University of Colorado at Boulder, where she received her MFA in Dance with an emphasis in video dance. Currently, she is an Assistant Professor of Dance and Video at Texas State University, where she co-founded Merge Dance Company in 2010.

Jessica Lindberg Coxe holds a BFA in Dance Performance from Southern Methodist University and an MFA in Dance Reconstruction/ Directing from Score from The Ohio State University. She has reconstructed and created Labanotations for four lost masterworks by dance pioneer Loie Fuller: *Fire Dance* (c.1896/2003), *Night* (c.1900/2004), *Lily of the Nile* (c.1900/2007), and *La Mer* (c.1925/2011). In July of 2005, the *Los Angeles Times* dubbed her work the "handbook" for historical dance reconstruction. The Fuller reconstructions have been performed by students at various universities and professional dance companies as well as the Art Institute of Chicago as a part of the *Toulouse-Lautrec and Montmartre* exhibit co-sponsored by the National Gallery of Art, Washington. She is a Language of Dance® (LOD) Specialist and currently serves as board secretary to LOD USA. She has been a professional advisor in dance education to the Dance Notation Bureau in New York City, and, in addition to notating the Fuller reconstructions, she has completed a commissioned Labanotation score of Doris Humphrey's *Grieg Concerto*. She currently teaches dance history, ballet technique, and modern dance technique at Austin Community College in Austin, Texas.

Ruth Grauert was described by the *New York Times* as "a witness to dance history." Grauert studied with notable choreographers Hanya Holm, Martha Graham, Anna Sokolow, Truda Kashmann, and Charles Weidman, among others. She danced for Nikolais as a member of the Nikolais Hartford Company from 1942-43 and in 1948 became his assistant and stage manager – positions she would hold until 1988. In addition, Grauert served as stage director for Murray Louis, Nikolais' long-term partner, from 1953-1970 and taught lighting at their Nikolais-Louis Foundation in New York from 1948-1995. Other credits include serving as lighting designer and stage manager for choreographers Phyllis Lamhut and Beverly Blossom, among others. Grauert is currently director of Bearnstow in Mt. Vernon, Maine, a summer arts institute she founded in 1946. She also has written widely on modern and contemporary dance, publishing numerous essays, articles, and reviews on dance aesthetics, education, staging, and lighting. In 2005, Grauert received the Martha Hill Lifetime Achievement Award. In 2009, she received an honorary doctorate from her alma mater, Ursinus College in Collegeville, Pennsylvania.

Kathy Dunn Hamrick, artistic director of Kathy Dunn Hamrick (KDH) Dance Company, received her BA in Modern Dance from the University of Texas and her MFA in Performance and Choreography from Florida State University. Between degrees, Hamrick studied in New York with Ruth Currier, an original member of the Humphrey/Limon Dance Company. She then taught at Florida State University, Stephen F. Austin State University, and the University of Texas; freelanced as a guest teacher and choreographer; and, after settling down in Austin, produced annual dance concerts for five years before forming her dance company in 1998. In addition to directing the KDH Dance Company, Hamrick teaches dance at Austin Community College, St. Edward's University, and at Hamrick/Warren, a professional modern dance studio located at Café Dance. She has taught creative movement to scores of under served elementary grade students and worked with foster teens through New Art Kinnections, the company's arts outreach program. She reaches out to hundreds of students each year by teaching master classes and conducting artist residencies in modern dance, improvisation, and choreography at Austin Dance Camp and for high school and university dance departments and dance companies.

Deborah Hay's mother was her first dance teacher, directing her training until she was a teenager. Hay moved to Manhattan in the 1960s, where she continued her training with Merce Cunningham and Mia Slavenska. In 1964, Hay toured with the Cunningham Dance Company for six months through Europe and Asia. By 1967, Hay was well known as a prominent young choreographer, and her unique style began to emerge within the aesthetics of Judson Dance Theater. Her many choreographic works include *The Other Side of O*, *Fire*, *Boom Boom Boom*, and *The Match*. Her works have been featured at festivals like Festival d'Automne in Paris. Her first book, *Moving Through the Universe in Bare Feet* (Swallow Press, 1975), is an early example of her distinctive memory/concept mode of choreographic record, and emphasizes the narratives underlining the process of her dance-making, rather than the technical specifications or notations of their form. Her second book, *Lamb at the Altar: The Story of a Dance* (Duke University Press, 1994), documents the unique creative process that defined these works. Her third book, *My Body, The Buddhist* (Wesleyan University Press, 2000) is an introspective series of reflections on the major lessons of life that she has learned from her body while dancing. Hay has received many awards for her work, including a NYC Bessie award in 2004 and a BAXten Award in 2007, and grants, including an US Artist Friends Fellowship and a 2011 artist's grant from the Foundation for Contemporary Arts. She also received an Honorary Degree of Doctor of Dance from the Theater Academy in Helsinki, Finland.

Peter Kyle is the Artistic Director of Peter Kyle Dance in New York City. An accomplished choreographer, teacher, and critically acclaimed performer (Nikolais & Murray Louis Dance, Mark Morris Dance Group, Erick Hawkins Dance Company, among others), he first encountered Slow Tempo in 2000 while working on a production of Ohta's *Mizu no Eki* in Seattle. In 2002, he accompanied P3/east to Japan to work with Mr. Ohta. He is among the first instructors in the United States to teach Mr. Ohta's work. Kyle teaches throughout the United States, including Sarah Lawrence and Marymount Manhattan colleges, and internationally. Kyle holds an MFA from University of Washington and a BA from Kenyon College.

Liz Lerman is a choreographer, performer, writer, educator, and speaker. Born in Los Angeles and raised in Milwaukee, she attended Bennington College and Brandeis University, received her BA in Dance from the University of Maryland, and received an MA in Dance from George Washington University. She founded the Liz Lerman Dance Exchange in 1976 and has cultivated the company's unique multigenerational ensemble into a leading force in contemporary dance. Lerman has been the recipient of numerous honors, including the American Choreographer Award, *Washingtonian Magazine's* 1988 Washingtonian of the Year, and a 2002 MacArthur "Genius Grant" Fellowship. Her work has been commissioned by the Lincoln Center, American Dance Festival, BalletMet, the Kennedy Center, and Harvard Law School, among many others. From 1994 to 1996, in collaboration with the Music Hall of Portsmouth, New Hampshire, she directed the *Shipyard Project*, which has been widely noted as an example of the power of art to enhance such values as social capital and civic dialogue. From 1999 to 2002, she led *Hallelujah*, which engaged people in fifteen cities throughout the United States in the creation of a series of dances "in praise of" topics vital to their communities. She created *Ferocious Beauty: Genome*, which premiered in 2006, with the participation over thirty scientists. The project has toured to sites throughout North America, including the Mayo Clinic and the Ontario Genomics Institute. Lerman addresses arts, community, and business organizations both nationally and internationally. She is the author of *Teaching Dance to Senior Adults* (1983) and *Liz Lerman's Critical Response Process* (2003), and has written articles and reviews for such publications as *Faith & Form*, *Movement Research*, and *Washington Post Book World*. Co-commissioned by the University of Maryland and Montclair State University, her newest work, *The Matter of Origins*, examines the question of beginnings through dance, media, and innovative formats for conversation. More information about Lerman can be found at danceexchange.org.

Andrew Long is a life coach and artist. He is a certified Hendricks Institute Life Coach and primarily focuses now on working with clients privately, through workshops, and by Skype. From 1990 to 2005, he was the artistic director of the Johnson/Long Dance Company. His original dance/theatre works in collaboration with Darla Johnson include *I Stuck My Head in the Garden* (2003); *Wait of Change* (1999), commissioned by University of Texas; *Grand Motion* with composer Darden Smith, commissioned by the Austin Symphony Orchestra (1999); *Atlas of the Universe* (1998); *Now & Again* (1997); *Walking on Water* (1995); *The Untouched Key* (1994); *9 Chains to the Moon* (1992); and *Till Human Voices Wake and We Drown* (1991). The company toured frequently, including Kampnagel (Hamburg, Germany), University of Hawaii (Honolulu), and Common Ground Festival (Los Angeles). Since 2005, Long has been the Director of Creative Arts Austin, a multidisciplinary arts organization that provides innovative arts programming to at-risk youth. Long is a sought-out teacher and lecturer and has been a guest artist at numerous colleges and universities in the United States and England. For more information about Andrew Long, visit www.andrewlong.net.

Nina Martin's choreography and master teaching have been presented throughout the United States and abroad, including Russia, Austria, Ireland, Finland, Lithuania, Italy, the Netherlands, Germany, Venezuela, Mexico, and Japan. Performance credits include Lower Left (www.lowerleft.org), David Gordon's Pick Up Performance Co(s), Mary Overlie, Deborah Hay, Martha Clarke, Simone Forti, PBS *Dance in America Beyond the Mainstream* program (dancing in the section featuring Steve Paxton), and Contact Improvisation. Martin has received funding for her work from the National Endowment for the Arts through six choreography fellowships, New York State Council on the Arts, New York Foundation for the Arts, Joyce-Mertz Gilmore Foundation, Meet the Composer/Choreographer Grant, Irvine Foundation (California), and the Texas Commission on the Arts, among others. She was a founding member of Channel Z (New York City), New York Dance Intensive, and Lower Left. She has served on the faculties at UCLA's Department of World Art and Cultures and New York University's Experimental Theatre Wing. Presently, she is a board member of Marfa Live Arts, which hosts the March 2 Marfa Performance Lab and Dance Ranch Marfa workshops in Marfa, Texas. She is also an assistant professor at Texas Christian University (www.dance.tcu.edu) and is continuing her Ph.D. studies at Texas Woman's University. Her article "Ensemble Thinking: Compositional Strategies for Group Improvisation" was published in *Contact Quarterly* in Spring 2007. Martin's improvisational systems receive a thorough examination in Melinda Buckwalter's book *Composing While Dancing: An Improviser's Companion*.

Lynne McNett earned a BA in Dance from Western Washington University and has over thirty years of teaching experience. For two decades, she has been teaching dance in educational settings, ranging from pre-school to college. She also worked as an adjunct faculty member at Western Washington University. Currently, she works as a professional development consultant for the Allied

Arts Education Project, where she trains dance art educators in teaching methods. She is on the Board of Directors for The International Association for Creative Dance.

Michelle Nance is an associate professor and BFA Performance/Choreography Coordinator at Texas State University. She enjoys teaching World Dance and Culture, Modern Technique, Jazz Technique, Composition/Choreography, and Productions at Texas State University. She is also active as a choreographer and performer. Her work has been commissioned and produced in Texas, New York, Colorado, Kansas, Minnesota, and Oklahoma. Some of the international locations where she has taught and performed include Scotland, Costa Rica, Greece, and France. Locally, Nance has appeared as a choreographer and performer with Austin-based REALMdanceproject, Forklift Danceworks, and the Shay Ishii Dance Company. From 1996 to 1998, she served as the Assistant School Director and instructor with the Erick Hawkins Dance Company. She holds an MFA from the University of Colorado at Boulder.

Julie Nathanielsz is a choreographer and performer now living in Austin. She trained independently in Seattle, Austin, and Amsterdam with Joan Skinner, Stephanie Skura, Deborah Hay, and Julyen Hamilton. She was also a member of the dance-theatre company Margery Segal/NERVE for eight years. She holds an MFA from the University of Texas at Austin. Her choreographic works have been nominated for several Austin Critics Table awards, most recently winning Outstanding Short Work in Dance (for *Working the Line*). In 2007, she founded The Meeting Point, an ongoing enquiry into performer (musician and dancer) perception in real-time performance. Her work has been presented by Fusebox Festival, Musical Bridges Around the World, Church of the Friendly Ghost, Salvage Vanguard Theatre, and the American Dance Therapy Association, among many others. She has taught at the Skinner Releasing Institute, as well as teaching improvisation and composition at Austin Community College and the University of Texas at Austin in the Department of Theatre and Dance. She regularly leads workshops.

Allison Orr creates award-winning choreography with all kinds of performers: from Venetian gondoliers to firefighters, trained dancers to Elvis impersonators, maintenance men to women over sixty-five. Defying easy description, Orr's work challenges audiences to expand notions of dance and performers while posing the question "who and what can be presented on stage?" Uncovering what is essential to the life of a community but often goes unnoticed is central in her work, as she seeks to give voice to people who may be marginalized or frequently overlooked. She was named Best Choreographer of 2003 and 2008 by the Austin Critics Table. Her most recent large-scale work, *The Trash Project*, was named the #1 Arts Event of 2009 by *The Austin American-Statesman*, the #1 Dance Event by *The Austin Chronicle*, and was awarded Most Outstanding Dance Concert of 2009 by the Austin Critics Table. Her work has been funded by the City of Austin, the Texas Commission on the Arts, the National Endowment for the Arts, The Austin Community Foundation, and the City of Venice, Italy. In 2005, she received a commendation for her work with visually impaired people from the City of Austin Mayor's Committee for People with Disabilities. In 2010, she served as a guest artist at the American College Dance Festival South-Central Regional Conference and was commissioned to choreograph the kick-off event for Austin's Fusebox Festival, involving over two hundred two-steppers on the steps of the Texas State Capitol. She is on the dance faculty of Austin Community College. She has taught a wide variety of students, including children, adults over sixty-five, and people with disabilities. Before founding Forklift Danceworks, Orr taught dance and studied with MacArthur Award winner Liz Lerman and performed with Robert Moses and Janice Garrett in the Bay Area. She received her MFA in Choreography and Performance from Mills College.

Carolyn Pavlik, assistant professor of dance at Western Michigan University, earned her MFA in Dance from the University of Washington in Seattle and her BA in Dance from the

University of Texas at Austin. She performed and toured nationally and internationally with the Austin-based Sharir + Bustamante Danceworks for thirteen years. In addition to the countless dances she performed by Sharir and Bustamante, Pavlik performed feature roles in Sharir + Bustamante Danceworks' repertory by noted choreographers Doug Varone, Ohad Naharin, Senta Driver, and Andrew Beckham. As a freelance artist, Pavlik collaborated with many Austin artists, including Kathy Dunn Hamrick, Margery Seagal, and site-specific dance choreographer Sally Jacques, as well as with Seattle-based artist Llory Wilson and San Francisco-based artist Kathleen Hermesdorf. She recently produced, choreographed, and performed for the camera works *Rack3* and *Genderations*. Her concert choreographic works have been presented in Austin, Seattle, and New York. She is nationally certified in massage therapy and Polestar Pilates. In 2004, she presented her research "Site-specific Dance in the United States" in the Impulses for Dance: Dance in the Community Conference in Portugal. Her site-specific dance research has also been published in the *Australia New Zealand Dance Journal*.

Peggy Schwartz is a professor at the University of Massachusetts Dance Department, where she teaches the Dance Education, Improvisation and Composition, and Yoga BA at the University of Rochester; the MS at SUNY/Buffalo; and MALS at Wesleyan University. She was the founding chair of the Dance Department at the Buffalo Academy for the Visual and Performing Arts. She regularly publishes, lectures, conducts workshops, and consults in dance education, curriculum design, national standards in arts education, and the work of Pearl Primus. She has presented at many conferences, including the Congress on Research in Dance, Dance and the Child International, and the National Dance Education Organization. Formerly, she was the associate editor of the *Journal of Dance Education*, a Board member of the NDEO, and a National Representative for Dance and the Child International. She received the Massachusetts Dance Educator of the Year award in 1994 and the Presidential Citation from National Dance Association in 1995. She was a guest artist at the Rubin Academy for Music and Dance in Israel, Scripps College, New York State Summer School of the Arts, and Pomona College. She was a consultant to the American Dance Legacy Institute on the work of Dr. Pearl Primus. She and Murray Schwartz, a literature professor at Emerson College, co-wrote the biography of Dr. Pearl Primus entitled *The Dance Claimed Me.*

Jennifer Sherburn returned to Austin after a seven-year stint of studies and work in the performing arts. Sherburn graduated from the University of Hawaii at Manoa with a BFA in Dance Theatre and received part of her degree at London Contemporary Dance School. Before the university, she studied at Austin Community College with José Luis Bustamante, Darla Johnson, and Allison Orr. While studying at Austin Community College, Sherburn ultimately decided to pursue a path in the performing arts. In 2007, she relocated from Hawaii to New York City to work with Troika Ranch Dance Theater as assistant to the artistic directors. She has continued to work with Troika Ranch over the years and is currently planning for their upcoming tour. While in New York, Sherburn freelanced for other companies, assisting directors, designers, and choreographers, such as 3-Legged Dog, Roland Gebhardt Design, and Jennifer Wright Cook. As a dancer, Sherburn has performed in many works around the country and abroad – most notably, works by Richard Alston, José Luis Bustamante, Betsy Fisher, Peggy Gaither Adams, Gregg Lizenbery, Alwin Nikolais, Johannes Weiland, and Pavel Zustiak. As a choreographer, she has premiered work at The Place in London; the Ten Days on the Island festival in Tasmania, Australia; an evening-length production at Marks Garage in Honolulu; and received a B. Iden Payne award for best choreography 2008 in Austin for *The Red Balloon*. In addition to work with Troika Ranch, Sherburn performs for Blue Lapis Light, serves as Artist in Residence for

Tongue and Groove Theatre, and continues to choreograph new works of her own.

LeAnne Smith is the director of dance at Texas State University and serves as artistic director of Opening Door Dance Theatre, founded with Karen Earl and Sandy Rodriguez in 1984. A graduate of Case Western Reserve University, Smith has danced the works of Erick Hawkins, Kelly Holt, Kathryn Karipides, Wendy Hambidge, Louis Kavouras, Joan Hays, and Karen Earl, among others. Her choreography has been presented in Ohio; Minnesota; Oregon; Washington, DC; Scotland; and Costa Rica. A recipient of the Presidential Award for Scholarly/Creative Activities, Smith continues to perform and teach throughout the United States.

Lauren Tietz is an improviser, teacher, dance-maker, and interdisciplinary artist who resides in Austin, where she has worked collaboratively with artists across mediums. Currently, she is finishing her MFA through Transart Institute, where she has focused on dance and the camera. She has been practicing Contact Improvisation (CI) since she was first exposed to it in 1998 in Arizona, and it has been a true love ever since. Her pursuit of more extensive CI training has taken her all over North America to study with such pre-eminent teachers as Ray Chung, Karen Nelson, Andrew de L. Harwood, Chris Aiken, Steve Paxton, Nancy Stark Smith, K. J. Holmes, Kirstie Simson, and Nina Martin with Lower Left. In Austin, she has performed and made new work since 2001. She has performed in the works of various choreographers, including Sally Jacques, Ellen Bartel, Caroline Sutton Clark, and Sumi Komo. She was a co-creator of the Improvisational Movement Project, a five-member collective of dance artists. She has produced multiple works in theatres and at specific sites in the city. She is currently part of the Meeting Point, a collective of dancers meeting monthly to research modes of composing dance in real time.

Nicole Wesley is a teacher, performer, and choreographer out of Austin. She received her MFA in Dance from Texas Woman's University and a BFA in Dance from the University of Texas at Austin. Nicole is a Certified Laban Movement Analyst (CLMA) from the University of Utah. She has performed works by renowned choreographers David Dorfman, Paul Taylor, Michael Foley, Donald McKayle, and Dianne McIntyre. Her choreography has been commissioned and performed nationally and internationally at performance venues such as the Dissolving Borders Symposia in Dundee, Scotland; Culturesfrance Danses Caraibe in Havana, Cuba; Dance City in Newcastle, England; the Big Read Festival in Austin; The Dallas Morning News Dance Festival; The American College Dance Festival; The MAD (Modern Atlanta Dance) Festival; The Fringe Festival in Costa Rica; The Fringe Festival in Austin; and The Fringe Festival in New York. She is currently an associate professor and the Program Leader of Dance at the University of Trinidad and Tobago's Academy for the Performing Arts in Port-of-Spain, Trinidad, and is Artistic Director of The JUSTICE Project with collaborative partner Darla Johnson.

ABOUT THE AUTHOR

Darla Johnson is a choreographer, teacher, and writer living in Austin, Texas. She was the co-artistic director of Johnson/Long Dance Company from 1990 to 2005, wrote for many of Johnson/Long Dance Company's (J/LDC) productions, and is a published poet. She is a contributor to Experiments in a *Jazz Aesthetic: Art, Activism, Academia, and the Austin Project* (2010, Omi Osun Joni L. Jones, Lisa L. Moore, and Sharon Bridgforth, eds.).

In its fifteen years, J/LDC received numerous awards and grants, including a grant from the National Performance Network and awards from the Texas Commission on the Arts, the City of Austin Cultural Contracts program, and the Austin Chamber of Commerce for its innovative cross-curriculum teaching projects in the Austin Independent School District. The Austin Symphony, the University of Texas, Dance on Tulsa, and Winona State University have commissioned dance/theatre works from J/LDC. The company performed nationally and internationally in such cities as Los Angeles, Honolulu, Little Rock, Albuquerque, and Hamburg, Germany, and taught residencies throughout the United States while touring.

Johnson founded the Dance Department at Austin Community College (ACC). In 1990, she brought her improvisation class to ACC, where it was instated into the college curriculum. Serving on the curriculum committee, Darla developed the curricula for ACC's Associate of Arts degree in Dance. She has created more than thirty works for the students and has directed and produced student choreography since initiating the bi-annual Choreographer's Showcase. She has received the ACC Teachers Excellence Award twice. In 2009, she received the National Institute for Staff and Organizational Development Award for Teaching Excellence and Service. In recent years, Johnson's work has also been produced and performed at the Edinburgh Fringe Festival; in Austin at the Black Arts Movement Festival; at Texas State University; at Spelman College in Atlanta, Georgia; at Georgian Court University in Lakewood, New Jersey; with the Shay Ishii Dance Company; and at the American College Dance Conference Festival.

The JUSTICE Project is Darla's current work and research project. A collaboration with colleague and collaborator/director Nicole Wesley, The JUSTICE Project has been commissioned by Spelman College, Northumbria University, The Contemporary School of Dance (United Kingdom), and ACC in Austin, where it received funding through a Big Read grant from the National Endowment for the Arts. The JUSTICE Project embraces the individual voices within the collective community. Using the concept of justice as the jumping off point, each participant writes and choreographs, sings, acts, or plays music in a personal expression of justice. Participants have collaborated and contributed works to be woven into the larger piece. The JUSTICE Project aims to enact social justice by the very process and creation of the work. The next incarnation of the project will be at The University of Trinidad and Tobago.

AUTHOR ACKNOWLEDGMENTS

I've never created in a vacuum. There are so many people I need to acknowledge and thank. I've had amazingly thoughtful and gifted teachers along the way. I particularly want to thank Liz Lerman, Celeste Miller, Deborah Hay, Pat Stone, Nina Martin, Terry Fredley, and Yacov Sharir. I must in particular thank Lucy DuBose, who believed in me and this book for the entire journey and who led me to Peggy Swartz, Peter Kyle, Ruth Grauert, Lynne McNett, and Mary Ann Brehm. I couldn't have done it without the support and feedback from Lucy Dubose, Annie Hartnett, Jessica Lindberg Coxe, Michelle Nance, Lauren Tietz, and Julie Nathanielsz. A special thank you to Jessica Lindberg Coxe for her detailed reading and feedback for the manuscript. Her input was invaluable.

Many dancers and performers I've worked with have been truly inspirational for me: Nicole Wesley, Jennifer Tietz-Gwin, Rudy Villela, Heather Sultz, Andee Scott, Kate Warren, Michelle Nance, Lila Geisler, Diana Prector, Cari Kerkoff, Rick Perkins, Bryan Green, Andrea Beckham, Amanda McCorkle, Layne Tanner, and Kristy Dixon.

To all my colleague and student contributors: this work would be incomplete without your voices and talents. I'm so grateful for your time, energy, and writings. I've had amazing students over the years who have helped me to develop this work. I want to thank Rachael Lieck, Kristi Melton, Melissa Watt, Leigh Gamon-Jones, Ramsey Foulk, Rebecca Ouelette, Elizabeth DeLeon, Nikki Johnston, Carissa Topham, Ashley Card, Molly Roy, Jennifer Sherburn, Debra McAdoo Schultz, Diller Schwartz, Betty Law, Amy Cone, Karen Morris, Suzanne Haberman, Bonnie Cox, Roman Morgan, Danielle Schreiner, Laura Noose, Maia McCoy, Tanya Winters, and Mimi Kayl-Vaughan. Special thanks to Lyman Grant, Dean of Arts and Humanities at Austin Community College, for the years of support for my teaching and creative endeavors. Thank you to José Bustamante for his support and the photos of our students.

If it weren't for the support and love of Tim Mateer and Andrew Long, I would not be the creator that I am today; my heartfelt thanks to both of these artists. To my sister, Donette Johnson, who has believed in everything I've ever tried to do, I have eternal gratitude and love. Many thanks to Kay Galvin, Jayne Krahn, Sara Breuer, Sheila Stricker, Charlotte Gullick, and Linda Rice Lorenzetti, my dear friends who supported me in times of doubt. I especially am so grateful to Curtis Gravatt, who gives me love and peace.

INDEX

Publishing

Established in 2004, TSTC Publishing is a provider of high-end technical instructional materials and related information to institutions of higher education and private industry. "High end" refers simultaneously to the information delivered, the various delivery formats of that information, and the marketing of materials produced. More information about the products and services offered by TSTC Publishing may be found at its website: publishing.tstc.edu.